The Disciples' Prayer

The Disciples' Prayer

The Prayer Jesus Taught in Its Historical Setting

Jeffrey B. Gibson

Fortress Press
Minneapolis

THE DISCIPLES' PRAYER

The Prayer Jesus Taught in Its Historical Setting

Copyright © 2015 Fortress Press. All rights reserved. Except for brief quotations in critical articles or reviews, no part of this book may be reproduced in any manner without prior written permission from the publisher. Visit http://www.augsburgfortress.org/copyrights/ or write to Permissions, Augsburg Fortress, Box 1209, Minneapolis, MN 55440.

Cover design: Tory Herman

Cover image © Gianni Dagli Orti / The Art Archive of Art Resource, NY

Library of Congress Cataloging-in-Publication Data is available

Print ISBN: 978-1-4514-9025-1

eBook ISBN: 978-1-4514-9661-1

The paper used in this publication meets the minimum requirements of American National Standard for Information Sciences — Permanence of Paper for Printed Library Materials, ANSI Z329.48-1984.

Manufactured in the U.S.A.

This book was produced using PressBooks.com, and PDF rendering was done by PrinceXML.

Contents

	Preface	vii
	Introduction	xi
1.	What Prayer Are We Praying When We Pray the "Lord's Prayer"?	*1*
2.	What Are We Praying for When We Pray the Disciples' Prayer?	*31*
3.	What Kind of Prayer Are We Praying When We Pray the Disciples' Prayer?	*41*
4.	The Prayer's Author and His Disciples	*63*
5.	Is the Disciples' Prayer an Eschatological Prayer?	*105*
6.	The "Temptation" Petition	*135*
	Conclusion	*161*
	Appendix: Was John the Baptist the Author of the Disciples' Prayer?	*167*
	Index	*171*

Preface

This book has its origins in two things. The first was a comment made by the late George Caird, my *Doktorvater*, to the members of the Theology Faculty of the University of Oxford when, in the spring of 1983, I was being interviewed for the Hall Houghton studentship in the Greek New Testament: namely, that my doctoral work on the Synoptic stories of the temptations of Jesus might result in resolving the long-standing and continuing debate over the meaning of the "temptation" petition in the Lord's Prayer. The second was the question posed to me on a wintry day by Robert (Bob) Jewett on what I thought the meaning of the temptation petition was, a question for which at that time I had only the vaguest of answers. In a very real sense, what I have written here is an attempt both to live up to the evident confidence that George had in me, to produce what he generously thought my doctoral work would lay the groundwork for, and to provide a better answer to what Bob asked of me than the one I initially gave him. So I must express my deepest thanks to them for providing me with the impetus to examine that aspect of the Lord's Prayer in depth, and then, as now seems inevitable, to branch out into a full-scale exploration of the meaning of the rest of that prayer.

But this exploration might never have come to fruition had it not been for the gentle but persistent nagging of my longtime friend Paul Griffiths to see it through. All too often I put the project aside. But every time I did, I always heard his voice echoing in the corners of my study to get on with things and complete what I had started. I owe him more than he knows. So I wish to dedicate this book to him. I hope he will receive it as a token of gratitude for his friendship over the years since we first met late in 1975 at Trinity College, Oxford, where we were undergraduates together.

Thanks too must be extended to teachers and friends and colleagues with whom I mooted, discussed, and debated the ideas fleshed out here, among them Norbert Schedler, Trevor Williams, Robert Morgan, Ed Sanders, and John Muddiman (who set me on my path of formal New Testament studies and also ended up with the task, after George Caird's untimely death, of supervising me as I completed my doctoral thesis), Tom Wright, Richard Pervo, Mark Goodacre, Stephen Carlson, James McGrath, Jimmy Dunn, Loren Rosson, Gail Dawson, Gordon Raynal, Carl Conrad, Troy Martin, and the members of Crosstalk: The Historical Jesus Discussion Forum and other online discussion lists, of the Chicago Society for Biblical Research, and of the Synoptic Gospels section of the Society of Biblical Literature.

Special thanks must also go to my editor, Neil Elliott, for his thoughtful suggestions for improving what I had set out in the initial drafts of this book. Any faults of grammar, explication, argument, and citation (or lack of it) that remain in the following pages are hardly his. I also thank copyeditor Jeff Reimer.

And finally I must acknowledge my immense debt to a person who in theatrical circles would be known as an "angel," my long-standing patroness, Margaret (Peggy) Pendry. Without her continued support over the years I would never have been able to have had the conference-based discussions with colleagues about the materials now included here that I have been privileged to enjoy.

Introduction

When you are praying, do not heap up empty phrases as the Gentiles do; for they think that they will be heard because of their many words. Do not be like them, for your Father knows what you need before you ask him.

> Pray then in this way:
> Our Father in heaven,
> hallowed be your name.
> Your kingdom come.
> Your will be done,
> on earth as it is in heaven.
> Give us this day our daily bread.
> And forgive us our debts,
> as we also have forgiven our debtors.
> And do not bring us to the time of trial,
> but rescue us from the evil one. (Matt. 6:7-13 NRSV)

Every day, Christians all over the world, taking the text of Matt. 6:7-13 as their cue, "dare" and "make bold" both privately and publicly to utter versions of the words that, according to the author of the Gospel of Matthew (and also the author of the Gospel of Luke) Jesus gave his disciples to pray.[1] But here's a vital question: *Do*

---

1. In the Gospel according to Luke the occasion of Jesus' giving his disciples what has come to be known as the "Lord's Prayer," or the *Pater Noster*, is not, as in Matthew, Jesus' desire to lay out fundamental and programmatic instruction for any who would follow him in the ways of the

THE DISCIPLES' PRAYER

Christians actually understand the words they utter? And here's another even more important one, one which lies at the center of this book: granting that Christians have *some* understanding of Jesus' words (as surely they must, especially if they have read studies of the this prayer or, as is likely, have been instructed by pastors and teachers on what the words mean), is this understanding in any way consonant with what *Jesus himself* understood the meaning and aim of his words to be? To put this another way: When we pray the prayer Jesus taught "us" to pray, are we really praying it as Jesus intended us to pray it? Is what *we* ask for when we petition God to let his name "be hallowed" and his kingdom "come," and for bread and forgiveness and for not being led into "temptation," really what Jesus thought and meant those he told to recite his words to be asking for?

Despite what many important students of this prayer think in this regard, I answer no. And in the following pages, I take up the task of showing, through an extended conversation with the bit of Scripture traditionally known as "The Lord's Prayer," that this is so.

God of Israel, but a request on the part of one of his disciples they be taught by Jesus to pray "just as John the Baptist did his disciples" (see Lk. 11:1).

1

What Prayer Are We Praying When We Pray the "Lord's Prayer"?

I begin this study with a question to which the answer is seemingly as simple as it is obvious, namely, What prayer are we praying when we pray the "Lord's Prayer"?

I say "seemingly" because in point of fact the question is more complex than it appears at first glance. And it does not have one answer. It has four. Moreover, unless one has a wide acquaintance not only with the way the prayer is actually prayed in all of the contexts in which people presently "make bold to say" it but also with the results of scholarly investigation of the prayer, these four answers are by no means obvious ones.

The first answer is this: the prayer "we" are praying varies depending on who one means by "we." The second is: we are praying a prayer that has been misnamed. The third is that we are praying a prayer whose English (and other modern-language) prayer texts are based on and derived from one of two primary and, in

1

substance and wording, divergent versions of the prayer;[1] moreover, even at that, most of these modern prayer texts do not faithfully reproduce the original form and wording of their source. And fourth, we are praying a prayer whose substance and wording, it has been argued, owe more to an early Christian author/redactor than to Jesus, even if it does originally come from him (see below). Let us examine each of these answers in more detail.

Versions of the Prayer among Different Christian Groups"?

Whether it is in private or within the context of public ceremony, all Christians are in the habit of reciting, sometimes daily if not more frequently, a scriptural text that has been named and known from antiquity as "the Lord's Prayer."[2] But the particular text of this prayer recited at any given time by any given Christian or Christian group is not necessarily the same as that recited by another.

Look at table 1.1 and compare the various ways the prayer is recited by British members of the Church of England, whose

---

1. The so-called Lord's Prayer comes down to us not only from two different places in the New Testament—from the section of Matthew's Gospel known as the Sermon on the Mount (Matthew 5–7) and from the section of Luke's Gospel known as the Travel Narrative (Luke 9:51—18:14)—but also in a longer (Matt. 6:9-13) and a shorter form (Lk. 11:1-2), between which there are verbal disagreements even at the places at which one has thematic counterparts with the other (on these, see below). It is also attested in a (most likely) early second-century-CE noncanonical Christian document known as the *Didache*, or *The teaching of the Twelve Apostles*: see *Didache* 8.2. On the date of the *Didache*, which some scholars have claimed is as early as 60 CE, see Kurt Niederwimmer, *The Didache: A Commentary on the Didache* (Minneapolis: Fortress Press, 1998), 57.
2. The origin of the title "the Lord's Prayer" lies, so far as we know, with the early Western church father Thascius Caecilius Cyprianus (Cyprian), a bishop of the North African city of Carthage between c. 246 and 258, who used its Latin form (*oratio dominica*) in the name of a short treatise on the prayer (*De dominica oratione*) that he composed in 252 CE. It does not seem to have been used in England before the Reformation, no doubt because, as Herbert Thurston has noted, from the Middle Ages until and even after the Reformation, the prayer was always said in Latin, even by the uneducated, who would have referred to it, as is still done today in France and elsewhere (especially within the Catholic tradition), by what they knew to be the first few words of the Latin text they recited during the Mass—i.e., *Pater Noster* ("The Lord's Prayer," in *The Catholic Encyclopedia* [New York: Robert Appleton, 1910], 9:356, http://www.newadvent.org/cathen/09356a.htm).

liturgical and private prayer life is formed and guided by the 1662 Book of Common Prayer; by Presbyterians, Lutherans, Baptists, and Methodists; by modern Episcopalians, using the text offered in Rite Two of the revised (1979) Book of Common Prayer; by English-speaking Catholics, who utter the prayer both privately and within the public context of the Mass in words set out according to the *Novus Ordo Missae*; and finally, by members of the English-speaking Eastern Orthodox communion.

1662 Book of Common Prayer	Presbyterian, Lutheran, Baptist, and Methodist prayer books	1979 Book of Common Prayer (Episcopal Church USA)	English-speaking Catholic prayer books	English-speaking Eastern Orthodox prayer books
Our Father,	Our Father	Our Father	Our Father,	Our Father,
which art in heaven,	**who** art in heaven,	in heaven,	*who art* in heaven,	who art in heaven,
Hallowed be thy name.	hallowed be thy name.	hallowed be your Name,	hallowed be *thy* name;	hallowed be thy name;
Thy kingdom come.	Thy kingdom come,	your kingdom come,	*thy* kingdom come;	thy kingdom come;
Thy will be done in earth	thy will be done, **on** earth	your will be done, on earth as	*thy* will be done on earth	thy will be done on earth
As it is in heaven.	as it is in heaven.	in heaven.	as it is in heaven.	as it is in heaven.
Give us this day our daily bread.	Give us this day our daily bread;	Give us today our daily bread.	Give us *this day* our daily bread;	Give us this day our daily bread;

THE DISCIPLES' PRAYER

And forgive us our trespasses,	and forgive us our **debts,**	Forgive us our sins	and forgive us our *trespasses*	and forgive us our trespasses
As we forgive them that trespass against us.	as we forgive our **debtors;**	as we forgive those who sin against us.	as we forgive those who *trespass* against us;	as we forgive those who trespass against us;
And lead us not into temptation,	and lead us not into temptation,	Save us from the time of trial,	*and lead us not into temptation,*	and lead us not into temptation,
But deliver us from evil.	but deliver us from evil.	and deliver us from evil.	**but** deliver us from evil.	but deliver us from *the evil one.*
For thine is the kingdom, The power, and the glory, Amen.				

Table 1.1

As we can see, among English speakers who pray the prayer known as "the Lord's Prayer," there is no universally agreed way of doing so. Nor, I might add, does there seem to be hope that such agreement will ever be reached. Members of the English Language Liturgical Consultation, a group of ecumenical liturgists in the English-speaking world whose mission is to develop liturgical texts for common use, standardized the text of the prayer, but the text they developed has been rejected by the very communions from whom members of the commission were drawn and for whom it was drawn up.[3]

---

[3]. See the entry for the Lord's Prayer in the English Language Liturgical Commission, "Survey of Use," 2015, http://englishtexts.org.dnnmax.com/ASurveyofUseandVariation/tabid/915/Default.aspx#thelordsprayer.

The Name of the Prayer

To state things boldly, the title conventionally used for the prayer texts outlined above is as inaccurate as it is without warrant—at least insofar as it is taken to be an indication that the prayer(s) known as "the Lord's Prayer" is *the Lord's* prayer, that is, a prayer that Jesus himself prayed. For although it is true (to paraphrase Heb. 5:7) that "in the days of his flesh," Jesus frequently "offered up prayers and supplications" to God, there is no evidence whatsoever that the address to God that we know as the Lord's Prayer or anything closely resembling it was, so far as we can tell from the Gospel record, ever one of the prayers that Jesus himself uttered. The evangelists place eight prayers on Jesus' lips (see table 1.2).

Matt. 11:25-26 // Luke 10:21

At that time Jesus said, "I thank you, Father, Lord of heaven and earth, because you have hidden these things from the wise and the intelligent and have revealed them to infants; yes, Father, for such was your gracious will." (Matt. 11:25-26)	At that same hour Jesus rejoiced in the Holy Spirit and said, "I thank you, Father, Lord of heaven and earth, because you have hidden these things from the wise and the intelligent and have revealed them to infants; yes, Father, for such was your gracious will." (Luke 10:21)

Mark 14:35-36 // Matt. 26:39

And going a little farther, he threw himself on the ground and prayed that, if it were possible, the hour might pass from him. He said, "Abba, Father, for you all things are possible; remove this cup from me; yet, not what I want, but what you want." (Mark 14:35-36)	And going a little farther, he threw himself on the ground and prayed, "My Father, if it is possible, let this cup pass from me; yet not what I want but what you want." (Matt 26:39)

Luke 23:34

Then Jesus said, "Father, forgive them; for they do not know what they are doing."

Mark 15:34

At three o'clock Jesus cried out with a loud voice, "Eloi, Eloi, lema sabachthani?" which means, "My God, my God, why have you forsaken me?"

Luke 23:46

Then Jesus, crying with a loud voice, said, "Father, into your hands I commend my spirit." Having said this, he breathed his last.

John 11:41-42

And Jesus looked upward and said, "Father, I thank you for having heard me. I knew that you always hear me, but I have said this for the sake of the crowd standing here, so that they may believe that you sent me."

John 12:27-28

Now my soul is troubled. And what should I say—"Father, save me from this hour"? No, it is for this reason that I have come to this hour. Father, glorify your name.

John 17:1-26

After Jesus had spoken these words, he looked up to heaven and said, "Father, the hour has come; glorify your Son so that the Son may glorify you, since you have given him authority over all people, to give eternal life to all whom you have given him. And this is eternal life, that they may know you, the only true God, and Jesus Christ whom you have sent. I glorified you on earth by finishing the work that you gave me to do. So now, Father, glorify me in your own presence with the glory that I had in your presence before the world existed.

"I have made your name known to those whom you gave me from the world. They were yours, and you gave them to me, and they have kept your word. Now they know that everything you have given me is from you; for the words that you gave to me I have given to them, and they have received them and know in truth that I came from you; and they have believed that you sent me. I am asking on their behalf; I am not asking on behalf of the world, but on behalf of those whom you gave me, because they are yours. All mine are yours, and yours are mine; and I have been glorified in them. And now I am no longer in the world, but they are in the world, and I am coming to you. Holy Father, protect them in your name that you have given me, so that they may be one, as we are one. While I was with them, I protected them in your name that you have given me. I guarded them, and not one of them was lost except the one destined to be lost, so that the scripture might be fulfilled. But now I am coming to you, and I speak these things in the world so that they may have my joy made complete in themselves. I have given them your word, and the world has hated them because they do not belong to the world, just as I do not belong to the world. I am not asking you to take them out of the world, but I ask you to protect them from the evil one. They do not belong to the world, just as I do not belong to the world. Sanctify them in the truth; your word is truth. As you have sent me into the world, so I have sent them into the world. And for their sakes I sanctify myself, so that they also may be sanctified in truth.

"I ask not only on behalf of these, but also on behalf of those who will believe in me through their word, that they may all be one. As you, Father, are in me and I am in you, may they also be in us, so that the world may believe that you have sent me. The glory that you have given me I have given them, so that they may be one, as we are one, I in them and you in me, that they may become completely one, so that the world may know that you have sent me and have loved them even as you have loved me. Father, I desire that those also, whom you have given me, may be with me where I am, to see my glory, which you have given me because you loved me before the foundation of the world.

"Righteous Father, the world does not know you, but I know you; and these know that you have sent me. I made your name known to them, and I will make it known, so that the love with which you have loved me may be in them, and I in them."

Table 1.2

It is true that two or three of these eight prayers look and sound as if they are snippets, or more accurately, echoes, of the words and substance of the "Lord's Prayer," especially, though somewhat ironically,[4] the prayers of Jesus found at John 12:27-28 and John 17:15. But these hardly count as evidence that Jesus himself prayed "the Lord's Prayer." What might be adduced as *sure* echoes of the prayer (i.e., the use of "Father" in his invocations of God, and the expressions "glorify your name" and "protect them from [the] evil [one]," John 11:41-43; 17:1-26) are both Old Testament formulations as well as forms of address and expressions typical of many ancient Jewish prayers. For instance, "our Father" appears in Isa. 63:16; 64:8; Tob. 13:4; and in several of the petitions of an important (though probably post-70-CE) Jewish daily prayer known as the *Shemoneh 'Esreh* or *The Eighteen Benedictions*, whose text we will explore in more detail below. The expression "Our Father in (the) heaven(s)"

---

4. I say "somewhat ironically" because it has been maintained, usually, as J. T. Robinson demonstrated ("A New Look on the Fourth Gospel," in *Twelve New Testament Studies* [London: SCM, 1962], 94–106, on the basis of the claim that the author of the Gospel of John, knew and used the Synoptic Gospels, that the sayings of Jesus in the Gospel of John have less of a claim to representing what Jesus actually said than those we find in Matthew, Mark, and Luke. For a contrary assessment, see P. W. Ensor, "The Johannine Sayings of Jesus and the Question of Authenticity," in *Challenging Perspectives on the Gospel of John*, ed. John Lierman (Tübingen: Mohr Siebeck, 2008), 14–33.

appears in Jewish prayers found in the Mishnah, the oldest authoritative postbiblical collection and codification of Jewish oral laws, collected and compiled by rabbis known as the tannaim ("repeaters") over a period of about two centuries.[5]

What we are praying is actually a prayer that, according to the evangelists who handed it down to us, Jesus taught his disciples (see Matt. 6:5-9a [cf. Matt. 5:2] and Luke 11:1-2a) and instructed *them* to pray (or to model their prayers on) in order, as Luke tells us (11:1-2a) and as Matthew implies, that they might specifically identify themselves, and be recognized, as his disciples. Accordingly, as such scholars as G. R. Beasley Murray, Donald T. Williams, Peter Doble, and Brad Young, have noted,[6] the true name of the prayer—or at least a more historically accurate and befitting title for it—might be "the Disciples' Prayer."[7] Consequently, throughout the rest of this book, except within my quotations of scholars who use the traditional designation, I shall refer to the prayer by this title.

The Source of Our Versions of the Prayer

It may come as a surprise, especially in the light of the importance that the Disciples' Prayer has had within Christianity, to discover that the prayer is given little prominence in the writings of the New Testament. It is not set out in any of the epistles attributed to Paul or Peter or James or Jude or John, let alone in the book of Acts or the Apocalypse of John. And although there is some evidence that

---

5. M. Sotah 9:15 and M. Yoma 8:9. On the Mishnah itself, see Herbert Danby, *The Mishnah* (Oxford: Oxford University Press, 1933).
6. Beasley Murray, *Jesus and the Kingdom of God* (Grand Rapids: Eerdmans, 1988), 147; D. T. Williams, *The Disciples' Prayer: An Intimate Phrase by Phrase Journey through the Lord's Prayer* (Eugene, OR: Wipf & Stock, 2005); Peter Doble, *The Disciples' Prayer: A Study Guide to the Lord's Prayer* (Peterborough: Foundery Press, 2000); and Brad Young, "The Lord's Prayer," in *The Jewish Background to the Lord's Prayer* (Austin, TX: Center for Judaic Studies Publications, 1984).
7. Indeed, Young goes so far as to remark that "the first barrier to a proper understanding of the prayer is the traditional title" ("Lord's Prayer", 1).

the authors of the Gospels of Mark and of John knew the Disciples' Prayer,[8] neither of them reproduce it in part or in full—a fact we will come back to later on when discussing the important issue of whether the prayer as we have set it out originates with Jesus. The Disciples' Prayer appears in only two places in the New Testament: at Matt. 6:9b-13, in the section of Matthew's Gospel known, thanks to Augustine of Hippo, as the Sermon on the Mount,[9] and at Luke 11:2b-4, in the section of Luke's Gospel known to Lukan scholars as the "Travel Narrative." Moreover, what we find at Matt. 6:9-13 differs in a number of ways from what we find at Luke 11:2-4. To see this, we need to set the texts of these two canonical attestations to the prayer side by side[10] (see table 1.3; note that the underlining of certain words in the Greek texts of the prayer indicates where the language of these texts differs in notable ways).

---

8. Cf. Mark 11:25 with Matt. 6:12 // Luke 11:4; Mark 13:38 with Matt. 6:13 // Luke 11:4; John 17 with Matt. 6:10 // Luke 11:2.
9. See book 1.1 of his exposition of Matthew 5–7, *On the Sermon on the Mount*, trans. William Findlay, in *Nicene and Post-Nicene Fathers*, series 1, vol. 6, rev. and ed. Kevin Knight (Buffalo, NY: Christian Literature, 1888), http://www.newadvent.org/fathers/1601.htm.
10. In reproducing and translating the Lukan text of the Disciples' Prayer, I have included an interesting variant of Luke 11:2, which speaks of a desired coming of God's Spirit rather than of the hallowing of God's name. According to such noteworthy scholars as Adolf von Harnack and B. H. Streeter, the variant stems from Luke himself and may have been an original part of the Disciples' Prayer. On this, see the important article by Robert Leaney, "The Lucan Text of the Lord's Prayer (Lk XI 2-4)," *Novum Testamentum* 1 (1956): 103–11. But not all agree. See, e.g., the arguments of E. F. Scott (*The Lord's Prayer: Its Character, Purpose, and Interpretation* [New York: Charles Scribner's Sons, 1951], 26–27) against the variant's originality.

THE DISCIPLES' PRAYER

Matt. 6:9b-13	Luke 11:2b-4
Πάτερ <u>ἡμῶν ὁ ἐν τοῖς οὐρανοῖς</u>	Πάτερ
ἁγιασθήτω τὸ ὄνομά σου	ἁγιασθήτω τὸ ὄνομά σου
ἐλθέτω ἡ βασιλεία σου	ἐλθέτω ἡ βασιλεία σου
γενηθήτω τὸ θέλημά σου	[ἐλθέτω τὸ ἅγιον πνεῦμα σου ἔφ' ἡμᾶς καὶ καθαρίσατω ἡμᾶς]
ὡς ἐν οὐρανῷ καὶ ἐπὶ γῆς	
τὸν ἄρτον ἡμῶν τὸν ἐπιούσιον	<u>τὸν ἄρτον ἡμῶν τὸν ἐπιούσιον</u>
<u>δὸς</u> ἡμῖν <u>σήμερον</u>	<u>δίδου</u> ἡμῖν <u>τὸ</u> <u>καθ'</u> <u>ἡμέραν</u>
καὶ <u>ἄφες</u> ἡμῖν <u>τὰ</u> <u>ὀφειλήματα</u> ἡμῖν	καὶ <u>ἄφες</u> <u>ἡμῖν</u> <u>τὰς</u> <u>ἁμαρτίας</u> ἡμῶν
<u>ὡς καὶ</u> <u>ἡμεῖς</u> <u>ἀφήκαμεν</u> <u>τοῖς</u> <u>ὀφειλέταις</u> <u>ἡμῖν</u>	καὶ <u>γὰρ</u> <u>αὐτοὶ</u> <u>ἀφίομεν</u> <u>παντὶ</u> <u>ὀφείλοντι</u> <u>ἡμῖν</u>
καὶ μὴ εἰσενέγκῃς ἡμᾶς εἰς πειρασμόν	καὶ μὴ εἰσενέγκῃς ἡμᾶς εἰς πειρασμόν.
<u>ἀλλὰ</u> <u>ῥῦσαι</u> <u>ἡμᾶς</u> <u>ἀπὸ</u> <u>τοῦ</u> <u>πονηροῦ.</u>	

Table 1.3

Now, as can be seen from table 1.3, Matthew presents the prayer as beginning with an invocation of the God of Israel both as "our Father" (Πάτερ ἡμῶν, *Pater hēmōn*) and as "in (the) heaven(s)" (ὁ ἐν τοῖς οὐρανοῖς, *ho en tois ouranois*) and then continues with seven petitions concerning, respectively, God's name, his kingdom, his will, his provision of the disciples' "bread," his contingent forgiveness of the disciples' "debts," the disciples' involvement with "testing" (πειρασμός, *peirasmos*), and their deliverance "from (the) evil (one)" (ἀπὸ τοῦ πονηροῦ, *apo tou ponērou*).[11]

---

11. The reason I have written "(the) evil (one)" here is that the Greek expression τοῦ πονηροῦ is ambiguous, possibly representing either the neuter or masculine form of the noun. It is unclear whether Matthew here (or John above) is speaking about "evil" in the sense of (1) "evil acts"; or (2) "that which harms"; or (3) an evil person, meaning someone who is wicked and is intent to perpetrate wickedness; or (4) "the Evil One," i.e., the figure who Matthew tells us put Jesus

Luke also presents the prayer as beginning with an invocation to God. But in his version this consists of only one word ("Father"). His follow-up to the invocation is a series of five petitions, the concerns of which are, respectively, God's name, his kingdom (or his Spirit/empowering presence), the disciples' "bread," the forgiveness of their sins, and their involvement with "testing," which sometimes differ substantially in form and in wording from their Matthean counterparts. For instance, Luke's representation of what Jesus told his disciples to ask God with respect to their "daily bread" is that God should "Go/keep on giving [it] to us day after day" (a translation that highlights the fact that here Luke uses the present tense imperative form of the verb δίδωμι, *didōmi*), whereas Matthew's is that God should "give [it to] us today" (a translation that brings out the force of the fact that Matthew's δὸς (*dos*) is the aorist imperative form of δίδωμι). Luke's representation of what Jesus told his disciples to pray with respect to receiving God's forgiveness is "And forgive us our *sins*, for we ourselves *are forgiving* everyone who is indebted to us," whereas Matthew's is "And forgive us our *debts* as/since we also *have forgiven* our *debtors*."

As should be evident, Christians who pray "the Lord's Prayer" in any of its contemporary liturgical forms pray a text that is primarily derived from Matt. 6:9-13, not Luke 11:2-4. In this, they are doing nothing new. They are, in fact, participating in a widespread and unified liturgical tradition that goes back to at least the early second century, if not before, and that is grounded in two things: First, the preference in the early church was for using Matthew's Gospel over Luke's as the source from which Jesus' teaching on any subject

---

"to the test" after Jesus was baptized and then driven by the Spirit of God into the wilderness (see Matt. 4:1-11). On this see the entry "πονηρός," in BDAG (= Frederick W. Danker, Walter Bauer, William F. Arndt, and F. Wilbur Gingrich, eds., *The Greek-English Lexicon of the New Testament and Other Early Christian Literature* [Chicago: University of Chicago Press, 1996]), 851.

was drawn; and second, the Matthean text is more symmetrical in its arrangement of its petitions than that of Luke, and therefore lends itself more readily to liturgical use than Luke's does. Note, for instance, both the balance in Matthew of the number of "us" petitions with the number of "you" petitions and the sonority of such words and phrases peculiar to his version as "Our Father" and "the one in the heavens" and "as in heaven, so also on earth."

But it also should be evident that what Christians pray under the title "the Lord's Prayer" does not, in any of the official ways it is prayed, faithfully reproduce the original form and wording of its source.

Most of this "unfaithfulness" in translation (if that is not too strong a description) is minor: for example, the reversal of the order of phrases in which Matthew renders the "bread" petition; the transformation of his use of the past tense in the forgiveness petition ("as we also <u>have forgiven</u> our debtors") into a present-tense formulation ("as we [presently] forgive . . ."); or the use in that petition of the word "trespass"—an expression that to us connotes encroaching without permission onto and violating someone's space, or even an actionable wrong committed against the person or property of another, as a proper translation of Matthew's ὀφειλήματα (*opheilēmata*), which, as we will see, denotes "owing something to someone."

But one such "infidelity" is major. That is the attribution to Matthew of a desire to end his version of the prayer with a particular doxology (a hymn of praise to God) that runs, "For yours is the kingdom and the power and the Glory, forever and ever. Amen." The doxology appears in all but the Catholic and Eastern orthodox versions of the prayer. True, the practice of adding this doxology to the prayer is also ancient. It appears to be first instanced in the late first- or early second-century-CE handbook on liturgy known as the Didache, or The Teaching of the Twelve Apostles, whose author presents a version of the Disciple's Prayer very close in form and wording to Matt. 6:9-13 yet ends, "For yours is the power and the glory forever. Amen" (see Did. 8.2).[12] As early as the third century, the addition was included in manuscripts of the Gospel of Matthew itself, as in a Syriac translation of the New Testament known as the *Curatorian Manuscript*, though here Matt. 6:9-13 is represented as concluding "For yours is the kingdom and the glory" (i.e., the expressions "and the glory" and "Amen" are absent). We also find the ascription to Matthew of a doxology in a sermon given by John Chrysostom, a fourth-century church father and bishop of Constantinople. To buttress a claim he makes about the majesty of God and the duties of obedience that Christians owe him, he adduces not only Matt 6:9-13 but also the specific words, "For yours is the kingdom, and the power, and the glory" as its scriptural warrant.

But the antiquity of the practice does nothing to mitigate the fact that the practice itself is an act of "unfaithfulness"—however piously intended!—in reproducing what Matthew presented as the text of the ending of the Disciples' Prayer. For, as many text critics have

---

12. Here is the text of *Didache* 8.2:

Πάτερ ἡμῶν ὁ ἐν τος οὐρανος
ἁγιασθή τω τὸ ὄνομά σου
ἐλθέτω ἡ βασιλεία σου
γενηθήτω τὸ θέλημά σου
ὡς ἐν οὐρανῷ καὶ ἐπὶ γς
τὸν ἄρτον ἡμῶν τὸν ἐπιούσιον
δὸς ἡμῖν σήμερον
καὶ ἄφες ἡμῖν τὴν ὀφειλὴν ἡμῶν
ὡς καὶ ἡμες ἀφίεμεν τοῖς ὁ φειλέταις ἡμῶν
καὶ μὴ εἰσενέγκῃς ἡμᾶς
εἰς πειρασμόν
ἀλλά ῥῦσαι ἡμᾶς ἀπὸ το πονηροῦ
ὅτι σοῦ ἐστιν ἡ δύναμις καὶ ἡ δόξα
εἰς τοὺς αἰῶνας.

On the relationship between Matt. 6:9-13 and the version of the Disciples' Prayer found at the *Didache* 8.2, see below, 26-27.

noted, citing our earliest manuscript witnesses to the text of Matthew (i.e., the fourth-century-CE manuscripts known as Sinaiticus and Vaticanus, and most of the Old Latin MSS, which lack the doxology), as well the lack of discussion of a doxology of any kind in our earliest written commentaries on the Matthean text of the prayer (such as that of the second-century church fathers Tertullian and Origen, and the third-century father Cyprian), it is certain that Matthew's version of the prayer originally ended with, "But rescue [or preserve] us from [the] evil [one]." In other words, the doxology was added to the original ending of Matthew's version of the prayer sometime after Matthew wrote, most likely, as many text critics and commentators have noted, to adapt the prayer for liturgical use in the early church.[13]

Anyone, then, who recites the doxology when reciting the Disciples' Prayer, thinking it is an original part of the prayer, is not reciting what Matthew originally wrote.

Did Matthew Get It Right?

What I mean by the question Did Matthew get it right? is this: Except for the doxology just discussed, has Matthew avoided doing what various liturgical texts do in their reproduction of Matthew's text of the prayer? That is, is what we find at Matt. 6:9-13 a reliable transcript of the words Jesus taught his disciples to use as the model for their prayers?

Many have doubted that this is so. One reason advanced for not taking Matthew's version of the prayer as a faithful reproduction of Jesus' own words is grounded in the widely held and reasonable belief that Jesus taught, and prayed, in Aramaic (or Hebrew), and not Greek.[14] This being so, would it not be inevitable, given that translation of texts into a target language are rarely exact

---

13. On this see Bruce M. Metzger, *A Textual Commentary on the Greek New Testament*, 3rd ed. (New York: United Bible Societies, 1975), 16–17.

reproductions of the sense and meaning of those texts, that something of the sense of the original wording of the prayer would be lost in its translation from Aramaic to Greek? Perhaps. But what happens if we assume, as many Matthean scholars assure us we should, that Matthew was not only, like Jesus, Jewish but also fluent in Jesus' purported teaching language? Would this not mean that fears of anything significant being lost in translation are groundless, and that we should consider that Matthew has indeed, albeit in Greek, presented us with an accurate and trustworthy representation of the prayer that he says Jesus gave to his disciples?[15]

Another reason for saying that Matt. 6:9-13 is not a reliable transcript of the words Jesus taught his disciples is one that, in the eyes of many, Joachim Jeremias established decisively as "fact"—i.e., that "it is clear" that Luke's version of the prayer is more original than Matthew's, at least with regard to length and form, if not, at certain places, to wording.[16] But is this true? To see whether it is or not, we need to examine the arguments Jeremias lays out in support of his claim.

---

14. But see Stanley E. Porter, "Did Jesus Ever Teach in Greek?," *Tyndale Bulletin* 44, no. 2 (1993): 199–235, who concludes, "It is virtually certain that he used Greek at various times in his itinerant ministry" (235).
15. We will return below to consider the particular and puzzling Greek word ἐπιούσιον (*epiousion*) that Matthew uses for the bread petition in 6:11.
16. Joachim Jeremias, *The Lord's Prayer* (Philadelphia: Fortress Press, 1964), 14. To be brief on the matter of wording, note, as Jeremias himself does, that Luke's "release/forgive us (from) our sins, for indeed we (our)selves now forgive everyone owing to us" seem less original than Matthew's "release us from the debts of us (our debts) as indeed we released/forgave the debtors of us" not only because of the abandonment of the parallelism between the use of the word "debts" in the first and second portions of the Matthean form of this petition but also because the abandonment appears to be in the service of making clear the meaning that "debts" had in a Jewish context—something that would not be clear if Luke was writing to a gentile audience, as seems evident from Luke 1:1-4 and other passages in his Gospel (on this see, e.g., the discussion of "Luke's Audience" in Robert Stein's *Luke*, New American Commentary 24 [Nashville: Broadman & Holman, 1992], 26–27). And his formulation of the "bread" petition, with its emphasis on a continuing giving by God of "our 'daily' [kind] of bread" day after day, also seems to many to be less original than the way Matthew sets it out. However, as I will argue below, it is probably a mistake to see the Matthean and Lukan versions of this petition as in any kind of tension with each other, let alone as having contradictory emphases or aims.

THE DISCIPLES' PRAYER

The first of these is grounded in something Jermias took to be "axiomatic," namely, that "what we have before us [in Matt. 6:9-13 and Luke 11:2-4] is the wording for the Prayer from two churches, that is, different liturgical wordings of the Lord's Prayer. Each of the evangelists transmits to us the wording of the Lord's Prayer as it was prayed in his church at that time."[17]

His second argument arises from his contention that the shorter form of Luke is completely contained in the longer form of Matthew. This, he says, makes it very probable that the Matthean form is an expanded one, for

> according to all that we know about the tendency of liturgical texts to conform to certain laws in their transmission, in a case where the shorter version is contained in the longer one, the shorter text is to be regarded as original. No one would have dared to shorten a sacred text like the Lord's Prayer and to leave out two petitions if they had formed part of the original tradition. On the contrary, the reverse is amply attested, that in the early period, before wordings were fixed, liturgical texts were elaborated, expanded, and enriched.[18]

He then goes on to note that the conclusion that the Matthean version represents an expansion of an originally shorter text is confirmed by three supplementary observations. To quote him:

> First, the three expansions which we find in Matthew, as compared with Luke, are always found toward the end of a section of the prayer—the first at the end of the address, the second at the end of the "Thou-petitions," the third at the end of the "We-petitions." This again is exactly in accordance with what we find elsewhere in the growth of liturgical texts; they show a proclivity for sonorous expansions at the end."[19]

---

17. Jeremias, *The Lord's Prayer*, 9–10.
18. Ibid., 11.
19. Ibid., 11.

Secondly,

> ... it is of further significance that in Matthew the stylistic structure is more consistently carried through. Three "Thou-petitions" in Matthew correspond to the three "We-petitions" (the sixth and seventh petitions in Matthew were regarded as one petition). The third "We-petition," which in Luke seems abrupt because of its brevity, is in Matthew assimilated to the first two "We-petitions." To spell this out, the first two "We-petitions" show a parallelism:
>
> > Our bread for tomorrow / give us today. Do Thou forgive us / as we forgive.
>
> In Luke, however, the third "We-petition" is shorter, apparently intentionally:
>
> > And lead us not into temptation.
>
> But Matthew offers a parallelism here too:
>
> > And lead us not into temptation/but deliver us from evil.
>
> This endeavor to produce parallelism in lines (*parallelismus membrorum*) is a characteristic of liturgical tradition.[20]

And third,

> ... a final point in favor of the originality of the Lucan version is the reappearance of the brief form of address "dear Father" (*abba*) in the prayers of the earliest Christians, as we see from Romans 8:15 and Galatians 4:6. Matthew has a sonorous address, "Our Father who art in heaven," such as corresponded to pious Jewish-Palestinian custom. . . . The simple *abba* was a unique note in Jesus' own prayers. Thus we must conclude that this plain *abba* was the original address.[21]

---

20. Ibid., 11–12.
21. Ibid., 12.

So, according to Jeremias, all of these observations lead us to one conclusion, that is, that the " . . . common substance of both texts, which is identical with its Lucan form, is the oldest text."[22]

And yet as convincing as these arguments have been for many, they are nevertheless extremely problematic. The first argument, as Brandt Pitre has noted, is simply a non sequitur: the presence of all the Lukan material in Matthew's version says nothing about its originality.[23] And the claim that "no one"—including, presumably, Luke—"would have dared to shorten a sacred text like the Lord's Prayer" not only is grounded in *petitio principii* regarding the nature of the text of the prayer but also founders on the fact that Luke seems to have no problem with altering "sacred texts," as his handling of Mark 9:33-34 and 14:22-25 shows.[24]

---

22. Ibid., 10–12; See also Jeremias's synopsis of his arguments in his *New Testament Theology: The Proclamation of Jesus* (New York: Scribner's, 1971), 195.

23. Brandt Pitre, *Jesus, the Tribulation, and the End of the Exile: Restoration Eschatology and the Origin of the Atonement* (Grand Rapids: Baker Academic, 2006), 135n9.

24. On abbreviating traditional sayings as part of Luke's style, given the rhetorical genre in which he composes, see Vernon K. Robbins, "From Enthymeme to Theology in Luke 11:1-13," in *Literary Studies in Luke-Acts: Essays in Honor of Joseph B. Tyson*, ed. Richard P. Thompson, Thomas E. Phillips (Macon, GA: Mercer University Press, 1998), 191–214, http://www.religion.emory.edu/faculty/robbins/SRS/vkr/theology.cfm. It should also be noted that not every student of the Disciples' Prayer shares Jeremias's view that no one in the early church, including the author of the Gospel of Luke, would have dared to shorten the Prayer. Here, E. F. Scott is exemplary:

"It might seem surprising that in spite of everything the prayer did not remain fixed, in the form given to it by Jesus. All Christians revered it as his, and one might think that the least departure from the consecrated words would at once have been detected and condemned. But it is always the best-known utterances which are most liable to be altered in common use. Every one makes them his own, and adapts them unconsciously to his own purpose. Familiar lines of Shakespeare are seldom quoted correctly. The hymn most often sung is 'Rock of Ages,' but there are no two hymn books which agree on the exact words, and all the versions are different from the author's own. We have to allow for this process of modification in the Lord's Prayer. Each company that prayed it was led to vary the words, so as to convey new needs by means of it, and this was in full accord with Jesus' own intention. He did not wish that the prayer should be said mechanically, as if there were some magical virtue in the words themselves. He meant that our own minds should be active, that his prayer should also be ours. It contained the substance of what we should pray for, and he left us free to change the form. *This was fully understood in the early church*" (*Lord's Prayer*, 23–24 [emphasis added]).

See too C. F. Burney, who speaks of Luke 11:2-3 as the "mutilated version" of the Disciples' Prayer (*The Poetry of Our Lord: An Examination of the Formal Elements of Hebrew Poetry in the

The second argument—which is the one most frequently taken up by those who argue for the originality of Luke 11:2-4—is false in two ways. In the first place, we have no evidence whatsoever that either canonical version of the prayer is a "liturgical text" or was ever regarded as such before the third century.[25] Nor have we any reason to believe that, even if the texts are liturgical, the "laws of development" Jeremias and others appeal to are real.[26] Where exactly are these laws on display in first-century liturgical literature?

The third argument, that all the Matthean additions come at the "end" of each Lukan petition, begs the question. How does Jeremias know that what he identifies as the "end" of each section of the prayer is actually its end, except by assuming the conclusion that Luke's version is the more original? Moreover, rather than being a sign of editorial insertion into a simpler text, the balanced stylistic construction in Matthew's version of the prayer may actually signal originality.[27] After all, did not Jesus himself employ parallelisms in his teaching?[28]

Finally, Jeremias claims that the Lukan version of the prayer is more original than Matthew's because Matthew opens his version of the prayer not, as in Luke, with the simple "Father" that was characteristic of the opening address of other prayers Jesus prayed (cf.

Discourses of Jesus Christ [Oxford: Clarendon, 1925], 112). For a full list of scholars who support the idea that Luke shortened a longer text of the prayer, see Shawn Carruth and Albrecht Garsky, *Documenta Q 11:1b-4* (Leuven: Peeters, 1996), ad loc.

25. Appeal is often made to Didache 8.3 to support this claim. But note that the admonition found at this verse to pray the prayer three times daily is to individuals, not a community, let alone a worshiping community. On this, see Niederwimmer, *Didache*, 138n26.

26. On this, see G. Schwarz, "Matthaus VI. 9-13/Lukas XI.2-4, Emendation und Rüchübersetzung," *New Testament Studies* 15 (1969): 233–47, esp. 233–34.

27. Indeed, it was the balanced structure in Matt. 6:9-13 which led Burney to declare that the Matthean version of the Disciples' Prayer, and not Luke's, is original (*Poetry of Our Lord*, 112–13). For more on the structure that Burney noticed in Matt. 6:9-13, see Ernst Lohmeyer, *The Lord's Prayer* (London: Collins, 1965), 25–28.

28. Ironically, Jeremias himself admits this. See his discussion of parallelisms as a characteristic feature of Jesus' way of speaking in his *New Testament Theology*, 14–20.

Mk. 14:36), but with a "sonorous" phrase ("Our Father who art in heaven") that closely adheres to "pious Jewish-Palestinian custom." But this argument not only too readily dismisses the fact that Jesus was a pious Palestinian Jew but also ignores that "sonorousness" is in the ear of the listener. More importantly, as already noted, the Disciples' Prayer *is not a prayer that Jesus prayed*. To say, then, that he would not wish his disciples to specifically address the God of Israel communally as other Jews did (i.e., as "Our Father") is to beg the question.[29]

In the light of these observations, I am less than confident that Luke is a better witness to the Disciple's Prayer than Matthew is. Indeed, I think there are good reasons for saying that Matthew did indeed get it right. But before I set these out, let us note one more objection to the basic reliability of Matthew's text—raised by several prominent scholars—that there never was anything from Jesus himself along the lines of Matt. 6:9-13 (or Luke 11:1-2) for anyone, let alone Matthew (or Luke), to reproduce.

The claim that Jesus never gave to his disciples anything like what we now know as the Disciples' Prayer—that is, a set of linguistically balanced strophes consisting of an address to God as Father and a series of connected petitions about God's name, his kingdom, his will, his sons' "bread," their debts, and a "testing"—was first given articulate voice some fifty years ago by British New Testament scholar Michael Goulder.[30] Goulder became convinced of his position primarily on the basis of the curious absence of knowledge of the Disciples' Prayer, even in its shorter Lukan form, in Mark's Gospel as well as in any

---

29. Moreover, the address "Our Father . . . in heaven" could be seen as vitally important, especially for Jews under Roman domination, if what Jesus was having the disciples do in the opening address of the prayer was to make a distinction between Jesus' reign and that of the Roman emperor, who claimed to be "Father" and was addressed as such in cult. On this, see below, 132–34.
30. See Michael Goulder, "The Composition of the Lord's Prayer," *Journal of Theological Studies* 14 (1963): 32–45.

other New Testament writing apart from Matthew and Luke, but also because of the fact that the Prayer is "preserved" in a different form in Matthew than it is in Luke. He then noted that none of the fundamental assumptions underlying the widespread scholarly claim that the Disciples' Prayer originates with Jesus "can be called satisfactory" and that "some of them are in fact highly odd."[31] If, Goulder asked, Jesus composed a prayer for his disciples to recite by heart (something Goulder also thinks was uncharacteristic of Jesus) and to pass on to others as a treasure to be guarded, should we not expect that the prayer would have been known to and used by other writing members of the early church? It would seem this would be especially true of Mark and John who recorded teaching that thematically is very close to the Disciples' Prayer (cf. Mark 11:25-26; John 7). And should it not be the case, given the presumed origin and the sacred quality and the intent behind the giving of the prayer, that when some did reproduce it, they would have done so in forms that were both consistent with one another and in conformity with what the disciples had ultimately passed on to them as one of the most important teaching that Jesus ever gave? And yet the prayer is *not* known to, or used by, any New Testament author other than the first and third evangelists. Moreover, its reproductions are, as we have already seen, at variance with one another. Furthermore, the form and language and emphases of the variances in Matthew's version of the prayer (i.e., the opening address and the petitions about God's will and rescue from "[the] evil [one]") are, as Goulder and others have correctly observed, as redolent of Matthew's style and theological concerns as the structuring and wording of the Lukan variances (i.e., the petitions about bread and forgiveness) are of Luke's. We have little choice, then, Goulder argues, but to conclude not only that

---

31. Ibid., 32.

both Matthew and Luke have felt free to make their own editorial contributions to the form and wording of the prayer but also that they too were not aware of Jesus ever having given anything like the Disciples' Prayer to his disciples. Would they really have had "the effrontery," Goulder asks, to change the form and wording of the prayer if it was indeed "the one piece of liturgy composed by the Lord himself"?[32] Would the churches for which (presumably) Matthew and Luke wrote have accepted, as they seem to have done, what would clearly appear to them as amendments to the prayer if, as the accepted history of the prayer assumes (i.e., that Matthew and Luke wrote no earlier than the 80s CE and perhaps, in Luke's case, much later), "the Prayer had been part of every Christian's catechism, and had been used (on a conservative estimate) for forty-five years?"[33] For Goulder, the answer to these questions is no.

The claim that the prayer as we have it now is not "dominical" has also been advanced more recently by John Dominic Crossan[34] and by members of the Jesus Seminar.[35] Crossan acknowledges that Matthew's version could have originated with Jesus. In its form and wording it is, he notes, citing Jesuit biblical scholar Joseph Fitzmyer, "a thoroughly Jewish prayer," and its opening address is consistent with the way Jesus seems characteristically, if not peculiarly, to have invoked God in other prayers the Gospels record him as uttering. Furthermore, Crossan believes the petitions fit very well as a prayer with what he believes is at the center of Jesus' mission, that is, the

---

32. Ibid., 34.
33. Ibid., 34.
34. See John Dominic Crossan, *The Historical Jesus: The Life of a Galilean Mediterranean Jewish Peasant* (San Francisco: HarperSanFrancisco, 1991), 293–94.
35. The Jesus Seminar is a group of about 150 critical scholars and laypeople, founded in 1985 by Robert Funk under the auspices of the Westar Institute, who set about with the express purpose of determining the historicity of the deeds and sayings of Jesus. With respect to the origins of the Disciples' Prayer, the Jesus Seminar follow Crossan's views on the matter See the seminar's conclusions on the historicity of the Disciples' Prayer in *The Five Gospels: What Did Jesus Really Say? The Search for the Authentic Words of Jesus* (New York: Macmillan, 1993), 148–50.

establishment, for an agrarian and often impoverished and oppressed community, of a radically ethical new way of living under the reign of God. This, Crossan remarks, "is especially so if 'daily' bread be taken precisely as such, that is, enough and no more material bread for one's daily needs, and mutual forgiveness of debts be taken precisely as erasure of monetary debts." In the Palestine of Jesus' day, bread and debt were the two most immediate problems facing the majority of the people Jesus addressed with his message of the dawning of God's reign—namely, the Galilean peasant, day laborer, and nonelite urbanite—and alleviation of these two anxieties were to Jesus "the most obvious benefits of God's reign."[36]

But despite these considerations, Crossan still finds it difficult to believe either that the strophe balanced prayer we find now at Matt. 6:9-13 or at Luke 11:2-4 was ever taught by Jesus to his followers, or, as some have supposed, that Matt. 6:9-13 represents a diverse set of miniature prayers later collected into one sequence.[37] Crossan's reasons are twofold. On the one hand, he thinks, as we have seen Goulder also does, that "if there had been a special prayer, specifically and emphatically taught to his followers by Jesus himself, I would expect an even wider attestation for it and also a more uniform version of its contents." But for him, the more important consideration is that "the establishment of such a coordinated prayer seems to represent the point where a group starts to distinguish and even separate itself from the wider religious community, and I do not believe that point was ever reached during the life of Jesus."[38]

---

36. Crossan, *The Historical Jesus*, 294, citing John Kloppenborg, "Alms, Debt and Divorce: Jesus' Ethics in Their Mediterranean Context," *Toronto Journal of Theology* 6 (1990): 192.
37. As is argued, for instance, by J. C. O'Neill ("The Lord's Prayer," *Journal for the Study of the New Testament* 51 [1993]: 3–25) and to some extent by Hal Taussig ("The Lord's Prayer," *Forum* 4 [1988]: 25–41).
38. Crossan, *The Historical Jesus*, 294.

THE DISCIPLES' PRAYER

For Crossan, then, as for Goulder and others, what Matt. 6:11-13 (and Lk. 11:2-4) "reproduces" is not something that Jesus gave to his disciples during the course of his ministry. Rather it is a postdominical creation, a summary, made by someone other than Jesus, perhaps Matthew himself, of the themes and emphases in Jesus' vision of the kingdom of God.

What, then, does this mean?

If Goulder and Crossan are correct, then there is absolutely no chance that what we find at Matt. 6:11-13—that is, a coordinated prayer consisting of an address to God as Father and a series of connected petitions about God's name, his kingdom, his will, the disciples' "bread," their debts, a "testing," and their "deliverance" from "evil"—represents something Jesus actually instructed his disciples to say.

But *are* they correct? I think not. In the first place, the idea that it went against Jesus' teaching practice to formulate extensive material that he expected his disciples to learn by heart seems, so far as I can tell, to be grounded not in what the evangelists record was Jesus' manner of teaching but in a question-begging assumption about who Jesus was, namely, a Cynic-style sage who taught primarily in brief aphorisms that were not necessarily meant to be memorized. But as we shall see below, how Jesus (not to mention the evangelists) seems to have regarded himself—and, notably, how others, including his enemies, saw him—was primarily as a prophet to Israel, much like such ancient figures as Isaiah and Jeremiah as well as, and perhaps more importantly, Jesus' contemporary John the Baptizer, who was speaking to, and dealing with, a particular national crisis on the basis of a particular theologically informed cultural tradition.

In the second place, the fact of our having no attestation of the Disciples' Prayer in New Testament literature written prior to (or even after) Matthew and Luke were composed does not necessarily entail the conclusion that the prayer was a "church creation." We know, for instance, from Paul that silence on what Jesus did and taught does not mean ignorance of what he did and taught. We also know from Paul that an author's not using "Jesus material" that presumably would have been useful has explanations other than that the "useful" material was not dominical.

Third, the argument that if Jesus had taught the prayer, it would have been more uniform in content than it now appears in its reproduction in the Synoptic tradition assumes that dominical words of great significance would not have been expanded or summarized by those who passed on those words. But this is clearly falsified by the Last Supper traditions.[39]

Finally, the claim that the prayer, in the tripartite form in which we have it (i.e., [a] address to God, [b] petitions in the second person, [c] petitions in the third person), could only have come into existence after the Jesus movement had separated from "the wider religious community" of which it was originally a part, which did not occur during Jesus' lifetime, surely begs the question. Jesus himself seems to have distinguished what he was calling his religious contemporaries to "believe in" and be faithful to as something quite distinct from what they thought being Israel entailed.[40] More importantly, it overlooks the fact that both John the Baptizer and the sectarians of Qumran, each of whom saw themselves as remaining a part of, if not the faithful (Isaianic?) remnant within, first-century Judaism, taught distinctive prayers to those who committed themselves to their understanding of what the God of Israel required of his people.

---

39. Pitre, *Jesus, the Tribulation, and the End of the Exile*, 154n61.
40. Note how this plays out, not only in Jesus' call to Israel to repent and to follow "the gospel" that he was announcing and enacting (why repent if they were already following what God has called Israel to follow?), but also in his characterization of his Jewish contemporaries who opposed him as an "evil and adulterous generation" (see Mark 8:12 // Matt. 16:4 // Luke 11:29; cf. Matt. 12:39) and who aligned themselves with, and taught, "the things of men" and not "the things of God" (Mark 8:33 // Matt. 16:23).

THE DISCIPLES' PRAYER

In the light of these considerations, there seems little reason to doubt that Jesus did indeed give his disciples something very much along the lines of what Matthew reproduces at Matt. 6:9-13. But can we then go on to say that what we find at Matt. 6:9-13 is an accurate and trustworthy reproduction of it? I think we can, though there is one objection to this conclusion that first needs to be dealt with before we can assert it with confidence. This is the observation, already noted above in our discussion of Goulder's view of the origins of the Disciples' Prayer, that the form and wording of what is peculiar to Matt. 6:9-11 are strikingly consistent with, and reflective of, Matthew's peculiar writing style and characteristic vocabulary.[41] But where does Matthew's style and vocabulary come from? Might it not be a reproduction, albeit in Greek, of the style and vocabulary of Jesus? This, ironically, seems to be suggested by Jeremias's analysis of the reliability of the tradition of the sayings of Jesus and the style of speech that Jesus preferred to use in the course of his ministry.[42] And if so, then another of the objections to the originality of Matthew's version of the Disciples' Prayer falls to the ground.

As to positive evidence that Matthew's version of the prayer faithfully represents the words of Jesus, we should consider two

---

41. On Matthew's style and vocabulary, see W. C. Allen, *A Critical and Exegetical Commentary on the Gospel According to St. Matthew*, 3rd ed., International Critical Commentary (Edinburgh: T&T Clark, 1912), xiii–lxv, lxxxv–lxxxvii; Rudolf Bultmann, *The History of the Synoptic Tradition* (Oxford: Blackwell, 1963), 351–59; W. D. Davies and Dale Allison, *A Critical and Exegetical Commentary on the Gospel According to St. Matthew* (Edinburgh: T&T Clark, 1988), 1:72–96; Ulrich Luz, *A Commentary on Matthew 1–7*, Hermeneia (Minneapolis: Fortress Press, 2007), 22–41.
42. Jeremias, *New Testament Theology*, 1–29. Note the antithetic parallelism, which according to Jeremias, following C. F. Burney (*Poetry of Our Lord*, 83–84), is characteristic of the *ipsissima verba* of Jesus, that appears in a portion of the prayer that Jeremias claims displays Matthean editorial activity—i.e., Matt. 6:13 (καὶ μὴ εἰσενέγκῃς ἡμᾶς εἰς πειρασμόν / ἀλλὰ ῥῦσαι ἡμᾶς ἀπὸ τοῦ πονηροῦ). Is it an accident that Jeremias leaves this verse out of his listings on p. 15 in his *New Testament Theology* of the places in the Synoptic Gospels where antithetic parallelism in the sayings of Jesus occurs?

things. First, as E. F. Scott has observed, far more than Luke's version, Matthew's is wholly Jewish in character,[43] and the petitions that Luke omits are organic to the prayer. Furthermore, the prayer as Luke gives it seems to reflect an effort to divest it of its particularly Jewish themes and thus make it more intelligible to Luke's gentile audience.[44] Second, note that the reproduction of the prayer in the Didache is not Luke's version of it, but essentially Matthew's.[45] We may, of course, account for this, as many scholars have, by saying that Matthew's version of the prayer is the one that the author of the Didache would have been most familiar with.[46] But the dependence of the Didache here (or elsewhere) on Matthew is by no means certain. Strong arguments have been advanced against it.[47] And if the Didache is not dependent on Matthew for the version of the prayer, then we have independent evidence that Matthew did not compose or add to what he took up from the tradition. What is the likelihood that two authors, working independently of one another on a shorter version of the Disciples' Prayer, would make the same additions in the same places to this prayer, in wording that is as identical as it is? Moreover, even if Didache 8.2 *is* dependent on and derived from Matt. 6:9-13, it cannot be ruled out, without begging the question, that the author of the Didache views Matthew's version of the prayer

---

43. Scott, *The Lord's Prayer*, 26. So too A. H. McNeil, *The Gospel according to St. Matthew* (London: Macmillan, 1928), 76–77. For more on this, see below.
44. Scott, *The Lord's Prayer*, 26. On Luke's audience, see above, n17.
45. The version of the Disciples' Prayer found in Didache 8 differs from Matthew's in four places: (1) in its identification of God the Father as "in (the) heaven" rather than "in the heavens"; (2) in speaking of "our debt" being forgiven rather than "our debts"; (3) in using the present-tense form of the verb αφιημι (*aphiēmi* = "to forgive") in the forgiveness petition instead of the aorist (punctiliar past) form of the verb that Matthew uses; and (4) in including a doxology ("because yours is the power and the glory") at the end of the prayer.
46. In support of this conjecture, it is often noted that both Matthew and the Didache have the same Syrian provenance. But in the end, this means little.
47. See Niederwimmer, *The Didache*, 46–50, and now Aaron Milavec, *The Didache: Faith, Hope, and Life of the Earliest Christian Communities, 50–70 C.E.* (New York: Newman, 2003), 312–13, and esp. 693–739.

THE DISCIPLES' PRAYER

as he does—that is, as words that come from Jesus himself (see Did. 8.2a)—because he knew that that was in fact the case.[48]

So to return to the question with which I began this section of my study—what prayer text should we be saying if we wish to recite the actual (Lord's) Disciples' Prayer? The evidence I have marshaled strongly indicates that it is indeed Matthew's version of Jesus' words. I render these words, for reasons that will become apparent as we go along, as follows:

> Our Father, the one in the heavens,
> ensure that we "hallow" your name
> ensure that your reign "comes"
> ensure that your will is done on earth just as it is done in heaven;
> do indeed give us today our "daily" bread
> and forgive us our sins
> in the same manner in which we have forgiven
> our enemies
> and keep us from subjecting you to "testing"
> but rescue us from doing evil.

But having said this, I hasten to add that reciting a text is not the same thing as praying that text, let alone praying the text as Jesus intended it to be prayed. If we do not understand what the text means, if we have no comprehension of what it is we are saying and what it is we are praying for when we utter its words, we are simply making noise. A reverent noise, no doubt; even a beautiful one. But still, just a noise.

But more importantly, if we pray the prayer with *an* understanding of the meaning of its words, as surely everyone but little children do when they recite the prayer,[49] but with an understanding that

---

48. Scott, *The Lord's Prayer*, 30.
49. I should temper this remark somewhat in the light of David Crump's accounts of how his wife, when a child, was puzzled by why she should ask God to "lead a snot into temptation" and how his young son would pray "Our Father, Art, in heaven. Hollywood is your name" as he began his recitation of the prayer (*Knocking on Heaven's Door: A New Testament Theology of Petitionary Prayer* [Grand Rapids: Baker Academic, 2006], 95).

is different from what Jesus understood the aim of his words to be, then we are certainly playing *a* prayer, but we are not praying the Disciples' Prayer, at least as it was originally intended by Jesus to be prayed.

So here is the central question of this book: When we pray the Disciples' Prayer, are we praying for what Jesus intended his disciples to pray for, should they utter the prayer that he gave them? In order to answer this, we will of course need to establish what Jesus intended the prayer to accomplish. But before we attempt to do that, we must first answer another question: What *do* we think we are praying for when we pray the Disciples' Prayer? It is to that question that I now turn.

2

What Are We Praying for When We Pray the Disciples' Prayer?

The question I ask in this chapter should, at first glance, be greeted with a raised eyebrow and a look of extreme consternation. Isn't it true by definition that what we are praying for when we recite the Lord's Prayer is what we think we are praying for when we utter its words? When, for instance, I recite the first half of Matt. 6:13 (par. Luke 11:4), which I was brought up to believe meant "Please God, do not bring me anywhere near temptation," and think that what I am praying for is either deliverance from ever being confronted by the alluring prospect of pleasure or advantage received from doing what I know is wrong, or for the divine aid necessary to prevent me from succumbing to an overwhelming desire for a forbidden object once such a desire has laid hold of me, then that is indeed what I am praying for! When I give to the prayer's words about "daily bread" the sense, "Please ensure that I never go hungry" or, more expansively, "Please make it so that I do not lack what I need for my well-being," then am I not petitioning God to keep me from want when I say, "Give us this day our daily bread"?

The answer is yes. What we pray for when we say the Disciples' Prayer is what we think we are praying for. The object of our prayer is what we think that object is. But let me note that in saying this, I'm not saying very much. For the question we *should* be asking ourselves is whether our understanding of what we are praying for when we say the words of the Disciples' Prayer is true.

Our Prayer and Jesus' Prayer

By "true," I mean: in concert with the meaning that Jesus intended the words of the Disciples' Prayer to have. After all, the words of the prayer were originally his, not ours. Presumably he had something specific in mind when he spoke of "temptation" and "bread" and "God's kingdom," and what one would actually and concretely be asking for if one were to pray to God to let his kingdom "come." Do we know what that "something specific" actually was?

Certainly, we assume we do, because we believe that our understanding of the Disciples' Prayer has been informed not just by what we have learned words like "bread" and "kingdom" and "temptation" ordinarily signify to us, but by all that a long chain of church usage and interpretation of those words, which is assumed to go back to Jesus himself, has in one way or another told us those words mean.

But is this assumption well founded? Let's take a specific example. What have many of us been told about the original meaning of Jesus' words in Matt. 6:13 // Luke 11:4, which the KJV renders, "Lead us not into temptation, but deliver us from evil"? I daresay it's two things. (1) These words have something to do with calling on God to help us avoid having, or to overcome, the experience of being drawn or enticed or seduced by the prospect of pleasure or advantage into doing what we know is wrong. (2) The reason they have this meaning is that what Jesus meant by the key Greek word πειρασμός (*peirasmos*) was (and is) exactly what is conveyed to us by the word that, until recently, has been universally used to translate it into English—the word *temptation*.

But is this correct? I myself once thought so. But I came to think differently when, during the course of researching what the authors of the various Gospel accounts said about the nature and content of Jesus' "temptations" (e.g., Mark 1:12-13; Matt. 4:1-11; Luke 4:1-13; Mark 8:11-13; Matt. 16:1-4; Mark 12:13-17), I discovered that in Jesus' time (and long before and after it), the key word in these stories, the Greek verb πειραζειν (*peirazein*) in various forms, which was the verbal form of the Greek word *peirasmos* in this petition of the Disciples' Prayer, like the Aramaic word *nisan* that presumably stands behind it, never bore the meaning that its English gloss now does. It was never thought to convey any of the connotations that the word *temptation* has acquired. On the contrary, *peirazein* always meant, when applied to persons, what we mean by the word *test*, that is, either a fact-seeking "probing" or a "proving" that functionally had nothing to do with getting or causing or impelling someone to act in a particular way. Rather, this "proving" had the intention, or the effect, of determining either how a person would act in certain circumstances, or whether the character one professed or was known to bear was well established.[1] Moreover, in biblical writings, the word was almost always used to denote a particular kind of "proving" and "probing"—that which we find spoken of in such biblical texts as Genesis 22 and Exodus 17, namely, a test that is designed or works

---

1. On this, see Joachim H. Korn, *Peirasmos: Die Versuchung des Gläubigen in der griechischen Bibel*, Beiträge zur Wissenschaft vom Alten und Neuen Testament (Stuttgart: Kohlhammer, 1937). See, too, my essay "Testing and Trial in Secular Greek Thought," in *Dictionary of New Testament Background* (Downers Grove, IL: InterVarsity Press, 2000), 1207–10.

to reveal the nature and extent of a person's faithfulness to a covenant partner.[2]

What does this mean, then, with respect to whether our understanding of the petition "lead us not into temptation" comports with the sense of the words Jesus used? Unless we have good reasons to believe that Jesus was speaking in ways that were out touch with his times, indeed, that he was giving those words some sense and significance that would have been both unknown and, more importantly, unintelligible to those who presumably were meant to immediately grasp their import—and as far as I can see, there are none—what we have come to understand these words to mean is *not* what Jesus meant by them.

This raises questions about what we think we are saying and praying for when we recite the other petitions of the Disciples' Prayer. Are we saying and praying for what Jesus meant his disciples to be saying and praying for? If our understanding of the meaning of the "temptation" petition is wrong, might we not also be wrong—that is, not in concert with Jesus' intentions—about what we think we are saying and praying for when we say, "give us this day our daily bread," or, "God, may your kingdom come," "may your name be hallowed," and so forth?

If we are honest with ourselves, we must acknowledge that this is a very real possibility. In order to tell whether this is indeed the case, we will need first to (1) set out just what contemporary Christians generally think they are saying and praying for when they recite the Disciples' Prayer and (2) outline what Jesus' words would have been taken to mean in his time and cultural context. It is the first of these tasks that I turn to now. The second will be the subject of the chapters to follow.

---

2. On this, see Birger Gerhardsson, *The Testing of God's Son. (Matt. 4:1-11 and par.): An Analysis of an Early Christian Midrash*, Coniectanea biblica (Lund: Gleerup, 1966), 25–31.

Some Standard Christian Views on the Meaning of the Petitions

I am not a mind reader, so I cannot say with absolute certainty what any particular Christian actually thinks he or she is saying and praying for when he or she recites the words of the Disciples' Prayer. But one does not need to be a mind reader to know what many, if not most, Christians think they are saying and praying for when they recite this prayer. We are actually told what it means over and over again, in a variety of ways: in published sermons and popular expositions of the prayer; in church-sponsored study guides; and, perhaps most importantly for our purposes, in works meant to shape the way Christians think about the meaning of the prayer's petitions, for example, discourses about the prayer written by denominational spokespersons and seminary-trained biblical scholars, or declarations about the prayer in the official catechisms of major church bodies. From what we find there, certain things are clear.

- What Christians think they are saying when they address God as "Father" is that God is not only a personal being, but also at least as close by, as caring, as merciful, and as providential as modern fathers are expected to be with their children.[3]

---

3. For a typical example of this view, see W. Phillip Keller (*A Layman Looks at the Lord's Prayer* [Minneapolis: World Wide Publications, 1976]), who writes, "Wrapped up in this little expression, 'Our Father,' lies a whole dimension of intimate companionship between father and child, between God and me. It reduces all the complications of life to a very simple, though very special relationship. . . . I know assuredly that God is my father and I am the object of His constant love and attention. There steals over my soul the realization that His concern and care for me are never ending, that his patience and compassion and mercy and understanding are always extended to me. In every situation in life, no matter how unusual or adverse, there comes the quiet assurance to my heart that I am his and he is mine . . . [and so] we can come [to him] with the quiet assurance that He will be receptive to our petitions and appreciate our gratitude" (22–23). See, too, Adam Clarke's remarks: "The word Father, placed here at the beginning of this prayer, includes two grand ideas, which should serve as a foundation to all our petitions: 1st. That tender and respectful love which we should feel for God, such as that which children feel for their fathers. 2dly. That strong confidence in God's love to us, such as fathers have for their children. 3dly. That strong confidence in God's love to us, such as fathers have for their

- What Christians think they are praying for when they say, "May your name be hallowed" is either that God will act in such a way that everyone will recognize him as a holy being,[4] or, working from the impression that "to be hallowed" means "to be praised," that everyone, and not just Christians, will eventually give God the honor, respect, and worship he deserves.[5]

---

children" (*Adam Clarke's Commentary on the Holy Bible*, ed. Ralph Earle (Kansas City, MO: Beacon Hill Press of Kansas City, 1967).

4. E.g., The blogger Nathan Eubank claims that "God hallowing God's name means making the holiness of the name known to the nations" ("What Does "Hallowed By Thy Name" Mean?," *Nathan Eubank blog*, March 7, 2013, http://www.nathaneubank.com/2013/03/07/). See also L. Chouinard, who observes that "the first petition asks God to act in such a way so as to reveal his holy presence in the world, thus silencing his opponents and creating a renewed sense of reverential awe among his people" (*Matthew: The College Press NIV Commentary* [Joplin, MO: College Press, 1997], 128). It should be noted here that my (and others') use of the masculine pronoun with reference to the God of Israel is due to tradition. It is not a statement of belief—on my part at least—that God should be thought of as male.

5. See, e.g., the remark of Albert Barnes that "the meaning of this petition is, 'Let thy name be celebrated, and venerated, and esteemed as holy everywhere, and receive of all men proper honours.' It is thus the expression of a wish or desire, on the part of the worshipper, that the name of God, or God himself, should be held everywhere in proper veneration" (*Notes on the New Testament Explanatory and Practical*, vol. 1, *Matthew and Mark*, ed. Robert Frew [Grand Rapids: Baker Book House, 1949), http://www.ccel.org/ccel/barnes/ntnotes.iv.vi.ix.html. See, too, the claim of Bob Leroe, pastor of Cliftondale Congregational Church, Saugus, Massachusetts, that "to hallow God's Name is to recognize, regard, respect, reverence, profess and proclaim God as holy" found in his sermon, "Holy Is Your Name," *Sermon Central*, February 2000, http://www.sermoncentral.com/sermons/holy-is-your-name-robert-leroe-sermon-on-lords-prayer-48156.asp. Cf. Keller, *Layman*, 49. Likewise Arthur Pink, who notes that "the words 'hallowed be Thy name' signify the pious desire that God's matchless name might be reverenced, adored, and glorified, and that God might cause it to be held in the utmost respect and honor, that its fame might spread abroad and be magnified" (*The Lord's Prayer* [Grand Rapids: Baker Books, 2005). Also John Gill (as quoted by Pink): "In the use of this petition we pray that the glory of God may be more and more displayed and advanced in the world in the course of His providence, that His Word may run and be glorified in the conversion and sanctification of sinners, that there may be an increase of holiness in all His people, and that all profanation of the name of God among men may be prevented and removed." More recently, Thomas Watson: "To hallow, is a *communi separare*, to set apart a thing from the common use, to some sacred end. As the vessels of the sanctuary were said to be hallowed, so, to hallow God's name, is to set it apart from all abuses, and to use it uprightly and reverently. In particular, hallowing God's name is to give him high honor and veneration, and render his name sacred. Although we ourselves can add nothing to the essential glory of God, we honor and sanctify His name when we praise and uplift him in the arena of the world, revealing something of His awesome character and reality to the sleep-infested eyes of those who live without Christ in the world" (*The Lord's Prayer*, electronic ed. [2] [Escondido, CA: Ephesians Four Group, 2000]).

- What they think they are praying for when they say, "May your kingdom come" is either to be granted the gift of a profound inner personal and individualized experience of God's love, forgiveness, or empowering presence,[6] or the hurrying of God's establishment on earth of something that they have been taught properly belongs to the world's future—a promised end of all earthly misery and injustice, a reign of peace and well-being, the experience of heaven on earth.[7]

- What they think they are praying for when they say, "give us this

---

6. See, e.g., the comments of executive director of digital media and the theological and cultural steward for foundations for laity renewal Mark D. Roberts: "When I Pray, 'May your Kingdom come,' I am opening my life to the Lord. I am offering myself as a servant of the King of kings. I am saying, in effect, 'Lord, direct my life. I am here for you, ready and available. Use me for your purposes and glory.' My hope is that I will act in every situation in a way that reflects God's sovereignty over my life" ("May Your Kingdom Come Soon, Part 2," *The High Calling*, April 20, 2011, http://www.thehighcalling.org/reflection/may-your-kingdom-come-soon-part-2. See also Keller, *Layman*, 63: "When Jesus uttered the simple request to his Father, 'Thy Kingdom Come,' . . . He was inviting [God] to establish [God's] Kinship in the hearts and lives of men. In fact, when any human being utters this prayer, if it is done in sincerity, it conveys the request to have divine sovereignty, God's government, set up in a human life"; and William Hendriksen and Kistemaker (*Exposition of the Gospel according to Matthew*, New Testament Commentary [Grand Rapids: Baker Book House, 1973], 330): "Here the desire of the supplicant is . . . not only that the kingdom may come extensively but also that it may more and more be established intensively, that is, that he himself and all those already converted may increasingly acknowledge God in Christ as their sovereign Ruler." As Henri van den Bussche has noted (*Understanding the Lord's Prayer* [New York: Sheed & Ward, 1963], 89), this view, which is at least as old as Origen (see *On Prayer* 25) is grounded in a reading of Jesus' pronouncement at Luke 17:21 that "the kingdom of Kingdom is *among you*" as meaning "the kingdom of God is *within you*," a reading that the Greek text will not bear and which in any case seems improbable, if not impossible, in that at Luke 17:21 Jesus is speaking to those who oppose him.

7. See, e.g., R. B. Gardner (*Matthew*, Believers Church Bible Commentary [Scottdale, PA: Herald Press, 1991], 119), "[Here believers] ask God to usher in the endtime era of salvation in which all of life will reflect God's purposes." See, too, almost all modern scholarly discussion of this petition. Typical here are the remarks Hans Dieter Betz: "God's kingdom is eschatological; it is established in heaven but not yet, at least not yet fully, on earth. The arrival of the kingdom "also on earth" that is, its complete victory over evil, is thus the content of this petition" (*A Commentary on the Sermon on the Mount, including the Sermon on the Plain (Matthew 5:3-7:27 and Luke 6:20-49)*, Hermeneia [Minneapolis: Fortress Press, 1995], 390).

THE DISCIPLES' PRAYER

day our daily bread" is relief from present need[8] or, as is sometimes noted, for Jesus himself, envisaged as the bread of life.[9]

- What they think they are praying for when they say, "Forgive us our trespasses as we forgive those who trespass against us" is either a remittance of expected punishment for the sins they have individually committed or a release from any and all guilt experienced on account of them, since more often than not the pronouns "us," "our," and "we" are transmuted, consciously or unconsciously, into "me," "my" and "I."[10]

- What they think they are praying for when they say, "lead us not into temptation" is either what, as I have noted above, I once thought I was praying for when I repeated these words—that is, divine protection from experiencing or succumbing to the sinful

---

8. Note Luther's remarks that what we are asking for in praying this petition is "everything necessary for the preservation of this life" and not just food, but also "a healthy body, good weather, house, home, wife, children (*The Sermon on the Mount and the Magnificat*, trans. Jaroslav Pelikan and A. T. W. Steinhaeuser, Luther's Works 21 [Saint Louis: Concordia, 1956], 146). See too, e.g., J. M. Boyce's note that "this prayer is a simple prayer for the things which we have need of every day" (*The Sermon on the Mount: An Expositional Commentary* [Grand Rapids: Zondervan, 1972], 191) and the comments by H. D. M. Spence-Jones that the "bread" petition is "for earthly food, the means of maintaining our earthly life" (*The Pulpit Commentary: St. Matthew* [New York and Toronto: Funk & Wagnals, 1890], 1:232) and William Barclay that the aim of the petition is "for that which is necessary for the maintenance of life" (*The Gospel of Matthew: The Daily Study Bible Series*, rev. ed. [Louisville: Westminster John Knox, 2000], 199).
9. A view that goes back at least to the church fathers Origen (*On Prayer* 27.2) and Cyprian (*On the Lord's Prayer* 18.40).
10. See, e.g., how both of these ideas are combined by Pink in his remarks on what Christians ask for in this petition: "First, we ask that God will not lay to our charge the sins we daily commit (Ps. 143:2). Second, we plead that God will accept the satisfaction of Christ for our sins and look upon us as righteous in Him. Some may object, 'But if we be real Christians, He has already done so?' True, yet He requires us to sue for our pardon, just as He said to Christ, 'Ask of Me, and I shall give Thee the heathen for Thine inheritance' (Ps. 2:8). God is ready to forgive, but He requires us to call upon Him. Why? That His saving mercy may be acknowledged, and that our faith may be exercised! Third, we beseech God for the continuance of pardon. Though we be justified, yet we must continue to ask; as with our daily bread, though we have a goodly store on hand, yet we beg for the continuance of it. Fourth, we plead for the sense of forgiveness or assurance of it, that sins may be blotted out of our conscience and from God's book of remembrance. The effects of forgiveness are inner peace and access to God (Rom. 5:1, 2)" (*The Lord's Prayer*, 19–20).

enticements and hard travails that daily plague us,[11] or, if they are aware of the notion, put forward by some scholars that here the word *temptation* refers to a series of trials to which God's elect will be subjected when God's sovereignty is finally reestablished over the earth and the world rid of all rebelliousness—preservation from the final and potentially overwhelming "test of faithfulness" that they believe awaits Christians in the (near?) future (232).

It is not only Christians "in the pew" who think these things; they enjoy scholarly attestation as well. Consider how Herman C. Waetjen reformulates the prayer in *Praying the Lord's Prayer: An Ageless Prayer for Today*:

> Indwelling and ever present God!
> Our Heavenly Mother who has given birth to us!
> Our Heavenly Father who calls us into mutual activity!
> We hold you in awe and summon all to join us in honoring you.
> We gratefully participate in your reign as we support its expansion throughout the world.
> We affirm your will for justice and peace as we continue to work for their realization
> But keep on supporting us with the food we need for body and soul.

---

11. See, e.g., Boice, *Sermon on the Mount*, 189: "[This request is] for . . . spiritual victories." See, too, Spence-Jones, *St. Matthew*,: "[The petition] is a prayer against being brought into the fulness and awfulness of temptation (cf. ch. 26:41; parallel passages; Mark 14:38; Luke 22:46). As such it cannot, indeed, always be granted, since in exceptional cases this may be part of the permission given to the prince of this world. So it was in our Lord's case (cf. ch. 26:41, and context). The words are a cry issuing from a deep sense of our personal weakness against the powers of evil. Into temptation; i.e. spiritual. External trials, e.g. persecution, may be included, but only in so far as they are the occasion of real temptation to the soul." Gardner, *Matthew*, 120: "The final petition is a double request, one which seeks God's help in facing evil yet before us: Do not bring us to the time of trial, but rescue us from the evil one (or from evil). Here (as in similar petitions in Jewish evening and morning prayers found in the Talmud) trial and evil are equivalent terms and refer to everything that could endanger our relationship with God. In praying the final petition, we ask God to protect this relationship: Do not bring us into situations that might overwhelm our faith, but rather deliver us from every peril that awaits us (cf. 2 Tim. 4:18; 2 Pet. 2:9; Sir. 33:1)". Also Boice, *The Sermon on the Mount*, 205, who claims that the sense of this petition is "Keep us from wandering into paths where we will be tempted by the devil; but if he comes, keep us out of his clutches."

> Forgive our sins and out indebtedness, as we forgive them to others.
> Enable us to recognize evil and avoid its influence.
> Empower us for your service, but spares us from trials too great to endure.[12]

But, as I asked above, is any of this actually what Jesus meant his disciples to be praying for in the prayer he gave them? It is to this question that I next turn. I note in advance that we will need—for reasons that will, I think, eventually be evident—to take a somewhat circuitous route to come to the answer, but get there we will.

---

12. Herman C. Waetjen, *Praying the Lord's Prayer: An Ageless Prayer for Today* (Harrisburg, PA: Trinity International Press, 1999), 124.

3

What Kind of Prayer Are We Praying When We Pray the Disciples' Prayer?

We can't know what a thing is for until we first know what a thing is.
—C. S. Lewis

I confess that besides looking at library catalogs, reading books, and pursuing the academic databases dedicated to matters biblical for articles in professional periodicals, one of the things I did when I began my research for this book was to Google the expression "(the) Lord's Prayer" to see what material was available on the Internet. In doing this, I discovered two things: First, that there is a staggering number of expositions and discussions and analyses of the prayer—some old, some new, some written by scholars, many not, cast in a variety of forms (from treatises to sermon outlines)—that are accessible through a few clicks of the keyboard. And second, that most of these expositions, discussions, and analyses are grounded in the view that the prayer is not so much an address to God that actual people in a particular historical context were meant to utter, presumably (and as we will conclude) to secure certain needs, as it is as a compendium of Christian doctrine from which proof for, and illustrations of, "divine mysteries" are to be extracted.[1] Much the same could be said of the view taken by the authors of many of the popular devotional commentaries on and study guides to the prayer that have found their way into print.[2]

In this, they are doing nothing new. Such a view of the nature of the prayer goes back at least to the late second century, to the church father Tertullian. In his work *De Oratione* (which should be translated "On *the* Prayer," meaning this specific prayer), an address written around the year 192 CE to catechumens on how properly to pray, Tertullian spoke of this prayer as "an *epitome* of the entire gospel" (*ut re vera in oratione breviarium totius evangelii comprehendatur, De Oratione* 1.35). In speaking so, he did not mean, as some have surmised, that the prayer contains the essence of Jesus' teaching. Rather, he meant that it embodied succinctly the whole panoply of what he took to be essentials of the Christian faith as it had come to be understood among the orthodox of his time, and was a sort of miniature version of, and precursor to, the later creeds in which the church's dogmas were more formally set out. Further, as Kenneth Stevenson has shown in his recent book *The Lord's Prayer: A Text in Transition*,[3] a masterful survey of the central role this prayer has played in Christian catechesis, exhortation, and doctrinal exposition from the

---

1. Examples of this are too numerous to list. But see, e.g., the sermon titled "The Greatest Prayer Ever Prayed" by pastor of Grace Baptist Church in Decatur, Illinois, Jerry Shirley, *Sermon Central*, July 2006, http://www.sermoncentral.com/sermons/the-greatest-prayer-ever-prayed-jerry-shirley-sermon-on-lords-prayer-92958.asp. And the online essay by John Marks Hicks titled "The Theology of the Lord's Prayer," http://dsntl8idqsx2o.cloudfront.net/wp-content/uploads/sites/10/2008/05/lords-prayer.doc.
2. W. Phillip Keller, *A Layman Looks at the Lord's Prayer* (Minneapolis: World Wide Publications, 1976), is a good example of this.
3. Minneapolis: Fortress Press, 2004.

late second century onward, this view has continued not only to hold pride of place among Christians but also to be advanced as the proper lens for viewing the prayer.

The Nature of the Text We Recite

But this view neglects (or chooses to overlook) the fact that according to those who first recorded our text, and presumably to Jesus himself as well, the Disciples' Prayer is from first to last not a summary of doctrine or a miniature catechism, but a particular verbal, heartfelt, and purposeful act of human communication. As such, not only was it given by Jesus in a concrete historical context (first-century Palestine, under Roman occupation), but it is also just what it says it is: a prayer. As such, it is communication; it

- presupposes a prior relationship between those who engage in (or "send") this communication (in this case, Jesus' disciples) and the one who is intended to receive it;

- recognizes that the receiver of the communication (in this case, the God of Israel) is one who supports, maintains, and controls the order of existence of the ones who are engaged in this act of communication; and

- is performed with the purpose of having some effect on the person with whom one communicates.

If it is to be mined for anything, it is *not* doctrine or dogma, let alone prooftexts in support of these things or platforms for sermons about them. If it is read as a source of information, it should be, as I will demonstrate in the following pages, for what it was that Jesus understood the nature of discipleship to be and what he believed faithfulness to the God of Israel entailed for those who truly wished to be regarded by God as his "sons." Here a comment on the translation of the Greek phrase υἱοὶ θεοῦ (*huioi theou*), the interpretation of which will play a significant role in this work, is appropriate. Older translations rendered the phrase rather unselfconsciously as "sons of God"; the NRSV used "children" on the premise, surely correct, that Jesus did not mean to limit the circle of his disciples exclusively to men. But "children of God," while appropriately inclusive of both genders, implicitly gives to the phrase a sense that one is speaking of juveniles, which is, I contend, not at all Jesus' point. I will risk using the older translation "sons of God" in what follows, not to imply that the concept expressed in the Disciples' Prayer has only males in view, but to emphasize that what is being expressed is a relationship of adult responsibility: Matthew and Luke use the phrase υἱοὶ θεοῦ for those who are faithful to the God of Israel and who, in their faithfulness to the path of obedience that, according to Jesus, God has set for them to follow, mirror and magnify his nature and character (see Matt. 5:9; 6:45 // Luke 6:35).

But to say that the Disciples' Prayer is what its title says it is—that is, a prayer—doesn't really get us very far along the road toward understanding what *kind* of prayer it is.

One thing is certain. The Disciples' Prayer is *not* a Christian prayer. True, it is certainly *now* a prayer that is *used* by Christians and not, so far as I know, by members of any other religion.[4] But when the prayer was given, and when it was first prayed, there was no such thing as "Christianity" per se—that is, a religion that was, and which defined itself as being, something distinct from Palestinian (or

---

4. Though see below for Rabbi Israel Abraham's remark about how at home he thought Jews would feel with the prayer and the account from Baruch Graubard, late professor of postbiblical Judaism at the University of Marburg, of how he was able to recover a "token" of his Jewish identity by reciting the prayer while hiding from the Nazis under a false Christian identity in a Franciscan monastery ("*Kaddish* Prayer," in *The Lord's Prayer and Jewish Liturgy*, ed. Jakob Josef Petuchowski and Michael Brocke [New York: Seabury, 1978], 61).

as some scholars have called it, Formative) Judaism in which Jesus himself was an active participant. As we will see below, it is through and through a Jewish prayer. Its originator was Jewish. Its recipients were Jewish. Its theology is Jewish. And so is its form, if not also much of its wording.

Moreover, as Colin Brown has pointed out, developing points about the relationship between the prayer and the story of Israel that Michael Goulder advanced in his *Midrash and Lection in Matthew*,[5] the prayer is firmly rooted in Israel's Exodus, Sinai, and Wilderness Wandering traditions.

The first petition is best regarded as a restatement of the Third Commandment (Matt. 6:9 par. Lk. 11:2; cf. Exod. 20:7; Deut. 5:11). It gives positively what the Third Commandment gives negatively. In so doing so, it not only precludes taking the name of God in vain; it also emphasizes what is implied in Exod. 20:3-6 and Deut. 5:7-10 (the First and Second Commandments) concerning how one committed to the God of Israel must never become involved in giving allegiance to "gods" other than Yahweh.

The fourth petition of the Disciples Prayer " . . . recalls the coming to Sinai and God's provision of the manna" (Matt. 6:11; Lk. 11:3; cf. Exod. 16:15; Num. 11:4-9; Deut. 8:3; Ps. 78:24 f.).

The petitions for the coming of God's kingdom and for the doing of God's will extend and supersede what the Fourth Commandment says about the sabbath (Exod. 20:8-11; Deut. 5:12-15)—which, as Brown notes, " . . . anticipates the kingdom as the reign of God—and the remaining Commandments specifically directed at personal relationships (honouring one's parents, killing, adultery, stealing, bearing false witness and coveting [Exod. 20:12-17; Deut. 5:16-21])."

---

5. Michael Goulder, *Midrash and Lection in Matthew* (London: SPCK, 1974), 296–301.

Similarly, the fifth and sixth petitions for forgiveness and avoidance of temptation not only have retrospective and prospective bearing on the whole range of the Ten Commandments. They echo themes that are intimately interwoven with the history of Israel in general and the wilderness wanderings in particular as can easily be seen when we remember what is found in such rehearsals of Israel's early history as Ps. 95 and especially Deut. 8:2 f., which declares: "And you shall remember all the way which the Lord your God has led you these forty years in the wilderness, that he might humble you, testing you to know what was in your heart, whether you would keep his commandments or not. And he humbled you and let you hunger and fed you with manna, which you did not know, nor did your fathers know; that he might make you know that man does not live by bread alone, but that man lives by everything that proceeds out of the mouth of the Lord" (cf. Matt. 4:4; Lk. 4:4).

Thus, as Brown (following Goulder) states:

> What the Lord's Prayer does is to apply the themes by which ancient Israel lived to the life of the new Israel. It is thus a fulfillment of the Ten Commandments and the exodus themes (cf. Matt. 5:17 f.). At the same time it transforms the themes from external commandments into petitions with which the one who prays personally identifies himself. And thus the law may be said to be written in his heart (cf. Jer. 31:33) as in the new covenant.[6]

Thematically, then, the Disciples' Prayer is undeniably Jewish.

But again, in noting this, our understanding of the nature of the Disciples' Prayer is not increased by much. For, as Bruce Malina has demonstrated, there are seven distinct types of Jewish prayers, which he classifies according to their purposes.[7] These are:

---

6. Colin Brown, "Prayer," in *New International Dictionary of New Testament Theology* (Grand Rapids: Zondervan, 1981), 2:871–72).
7. Bruce Malina, "What Is Prayer?," *The Bible Today* 18 (1980): 214–20.

- "I want" or petitionary prayers, uttered orally or mentally by individuals or groups to obtain goods and services.
- "Do as I tell you . . ." or regulatory prayers, which aim to control the activity of God, to command God to order people and things about on behalf of the one praying.
- "Where are you when I need you?" or interactional prayers, which seek to maintain emotional ties with God, especially in times of distress or to restore a favored relationship that seems to have been disrupted.
- "I gave them your word . . . I kept them safe" or self-focused prayers, which aim to identify the self—individual and social—to God as deserving of God's acknowledgment and approval for having done what God requires of the faithful.
- "Tell me why . . ." or heuristic prayers; other examples are "Should I marry?" "take the job?" "refuse to fight?" These seek understanding of God's will for us or workings within us, individually and collectively, that at present seem inexplicable or in contradiction with God's ways.
- "I was caught up to the second heaven" or imaginative/contemplative prayers, whose aim is to create an environment of one's own with God and to maintain one's present relationship with God.
- "I have something to tell you, God" or acknowledgment prayers, which aim to praise, confirm, or publicly proclaim the recognition of God's sovereignty or glory, or to express gratitude and appreciation for divine benefaction.

So what type of prayer is the Disciples' Prayer? The answer becomes clear when we note two things. First, that each of its postinvocation elements is cast in the form either of a command or a request, and that these commands and requests are made to gain something from God. And second, that the prayer itself was grounded in Jesus' perception (1) of specific communal needs his disciples had because they were his disciples; (2) of securing from the God of Israel what was necessary to meet those needs; and (3) of its efficaciousness. In the light of this, it seems clear that the Disciples' Prayer is an "I want" (petitionary) prayer.

To show this more fully, we first have to come to a clear decision about two things: First, what Jesus thinks (or is presented by the evangelists as thinking) the needs of his disciples are; and second, what the disciples would actually be asking for when they addressed God with the prayer Jesus gave them. But since I won't be discussing these topics until chapter 5 of this book, we will have to wait a bit to see exactly what's what in this regard.

Is the Disciples' Prayer a Derivative Prayer?

I've just asserted that the Disciples' Prayer was a thoroughly Jewish prayer. Let's consider how this is so by comparing two sets of things:

- The understanding of God it attests to and affirms (albeit indirectly) with the confessions about God that not only were central to first-century Judaism but also distinguished it from all other religions in the ancient world (and, incidentally, for which many first-century Jews died or were willing to give up their lives to affirm).

- The form and language of the prayer with that of (allegedly: see below) first-century Jewish prayers.

As we've had more than one occasion to observe, the Disciples' Prayer begins with an address to the God of Israel (a fact that is in itself sufficient for showing that the prayer is a Jewish prayer), in which this God is invoked as "Father." In this, it is at one with first-century Jews whose ancient traditions, along with the prophets, taught them not only to view their God as Father (see Exod. 4:22; Hosea 11:1; Jer. 31:9; Isa. 63:16; 64:7) but also to proclaim him as such, especially in prayer (see Tob. 13:4; Sir. 51:10; Wis. 14:3; 4Q372 1:16).[8]

The Disciples' Prayer also views God as vitally concerned with the holiness of his name. In this it mirrors, and seems consciously to draw on, the Jewish understanding of God proclaimed in Isa. 29:23 and Ezek. 36:23-3, 7, as one who will ensure that his name is hallowed and who takes great umbrage when his people profane it.

The Disciples' Prayer recognizes not only that God has a people, but also that he alone is to be King over them. This is a tenet of Jewish theology so vital to the life of Judaism that when non-Jews such as the Greek king of Syria Antiochus Epiphanes and the Roman emperor Caligula dared to challenge it or prevent it from being acknowledged, they fermented grave social unrest and costly revolts against themselves.[9] Furthermore, the Disciples' Prayer presupposes, especially in the "kingdom" petition, that the God of Israel has given his people a concrete hope that he intends to decisively establish his sovereignty over all those who have rebelled against him, just as such Jewish texts as the Psalms of Solomon and many of the Dead Sea Scrolls declare he has.

---

8. On this, contra claims associated with Joachim Jeremias and his followers that Jesus was distinct in this, see J. M. Oesterreicher, "'Abba, Father!' On the Humanity of Jesus," in Petuchowski and Brocke, *The Lord's Prayer and Jewish Liturgy*, 122–34. For a succinct yet telling account of the rise, use, influence, and fall of Jeremias's view, see David Crump, *Knocking on Heaven's Door: A New Testament Theology of Petitionary Prayer* (Grand Rapids: Baker Academic, 2006), 97–99.

9. On the revolution fermented by Antiochus IV Epiphanes efforts to force Jews to worship gods other than Yahweh, see 1 and 2 Maccabees. See too Daniel J. Harrington, *The Maccabean Revolt: Anatomy of a Biblical Revolution* (Wilmington, DE: Michael Glazier, 1991). On the consequences of the attempts of Caligula to install a statue of himself (as Zeus) in the Jerusalem temple, see Josephus, *Jewish War* 185; *Antiquities of the Jews* 18.272-274.

Finally, the Disciples' Prayer expresses a fervent belief that God provides for and forgives those who remain faithful to him—a mainstay in Jewish theology. Indeed, so consistent and consonant with the Jewish understanding of God is the theology of the Disciples' Prayer that after reading and studying it, a prominent Jewish rabbinic scholar, Israel Abrahams, found himself compelled to proclaim that no Jew would ever be averse to making this prayer his or her own prayer![10]

But it is not just in its theology that the prayer is Jewish. It is Jewish in its form and in its language. Formally, the structure of the Disciples' Prayer follows (up to a point) the tripartite scheme of "praise—petitions—thanksgiving" found in many ancient Jewish prayers, especially (so it will be argued below) that of the one many Jews call *the* prayer, namely, the Amidah. This prayer, which is also known as the Shemoneh Esreh or the Eighteen Benedictions, became, sometime in the first century CE, the primary prayer of both public and private Jewish worship. It stands now as the center of the Mussaf ("Additional") service, which is recited on Shabbat (Jewish Sabbath), Rosh Chodesh (New Moon), and other Jewish festivals, after the morning Torah reading. As Joseph Heineman, one of the foremost authorities on ancient Jewish prayer, has noted, the Disciples' Prayer displays all of the characteristics of what he calls the Jewish "short/private" prayer, an example of which is the prayer of Eliezer found in b. Ber. 29b.[11] It reads:

> Do your will in heaven above, and grant relief to them that fear you below and do that which is good in your eyes. Blessed are you, O Lord, who hears prayer. You, O Lord, who hearkens to prayer.

---

10. Israel Abrahams, "The Lord's Prayer," in *Studies in Pharisaism and the Gospels* (Cambridge: Cambridge University Press, 1924), second series, 97.
11. The Babylonian Talmud (b.) is a record of rabbinic discussions pertaining to Jewish law, ethics, customs, and history that was compiled in Babylon in the sixth century CE. Berakoth (or Blessings) is one tractate in the Talmud.

Another is the prayer of a rabbi named Joshua that appears in m. Ber. 4:4:[12]

> God, save your nation, Israel. In all critical times let their needs be before you. Blessed are you, O God, who hearkens to prayer.

As these prayers do, the Disciples' Prayer also employs a form of one of the epithets used frequently in private petitions. It, too, addresses God in the second person. It possesses the same simple style as we find in these "brief" Jewish prayers—a style that, incidentally, was thought to be an indication of a sense of danger on the part of the pray-er[13]—and, like these prayers, it is in toto brief in length, as are its component sentences.

As to its linguistic similarities with Jewish prayers, consider four things. First, observe the rough similarity of the wording of the "name" and "kingdom" clauses of the Disciples' Prayer with the wording of the Jewish prayer known as the Kaddish, a doxology that was originally recited, with congregational responses, at the close of the prayers in the synagogue, and now is frequently recited after Scripture readings and religious discourses in schoolhouse or synagogue:[14]

> Exalted and sanctified is God's great name
> in the world which He has created according to His will
> and may He establish His kingdom
> in your lifetime and your days
> and in the lifetimes of all the House of Israel
> speedily and soon.

---

12. The Mishnah (m.) is the first major compiling into written form of the Oral Torah—the legal and interpretative traditions about the meaning of the legal materials in the Pentateuch that, according to tradition, were passed down from Moses by sages in an unbroken chain of transmission that ended with the second-century-CE rabbi known as Judah the Prince. The Mishnah also includes a tractate Berakoth.
13. Joseph Heineman, *Prayer in the Talmud*, Studia Judaica 9 (Berlin: de Gruyter, 1977), 188.
14. On this, see Jakob Josef Petuchowski and Michael Brocke, introduction to B. Gebraud, "The Kaddish Prayer," in Petuchowski and Brocke, *The Lord's Prayer and the Jewish Liturgy*, 59–61.

> May His great name be blessed
> forever and to all eternity.
> Blessed and praised, glorified and exalted
> extolled and honored, elevated and lauded.

Second, note the linguistic similarity of these same clauses with the wording of the eleventh petition of what appears to be an early form of the Amidah:

> Restore our judges as at first
> and our counselors as in the beginning,
> (and remove from us sorrow and sighing)
> and you yourself reign over us, you alone
> (with loving kindness and compassion),
> and clear us in judgment.
> (Blessed are you, O Lord, the King
> who loves righteousness and justice).
> Blessed are you, Lord, who loves justice.

Consider, third, how closely Jesus' words about forgiveness and forgiving in the Disciples' Prayer seem to echo the sixth petition of the Amidah, which asks God "our Father":

> Forgive us, our Father, for we have sinned; pardon us, our King, for we have rebelled; for You are a pardoner and a forgiver. Blessed are you, Lord, the gracious One who abundantly forgives.

And fourth, consider how close the wording of the so-called "temptation" clause of the Disciples' Prayer (Matt. 6:13a // Luke 11:4b) is to that of the following lines of the Jewish Morning Prayer (preserved in Ber. 60b):

> and lead me not into sin [*Lo l'yidei ḥet*],
> or into iniquity [*'avon*]
> or into testing [*ni'sa'yon*],
> or into contempt [*biza'yon*].

In the light of all of this, it is hard to think that the Disciples' Prayer is anything other than a Jewish prayer.

But this raises a question. Does the Jewishness of the Disciples' Prayer mean that the Disciples' Prayer is a derivative prayer? That is to say, given how closely the Disciples' Prayer seems to mirror, if not employ, the form and language of the Jewish prayers I've noted, was it cobbled together from the prayers that it formally and linguistically resembles?

This is an important question. It touches on the issue of the originality of the prayer—though this is in the end something of a side issue, since we have no reason, other than the questionable and possibly antisemitic a priori view that Jesus was (or had to be) unique among, if not superior to, his coreligionists, to expect that Jesus was (always, and even here) wholly original in what he taught. Indeed, the desire on the part of Christians that he should have been unique seems to betray a strange but not unprecedented wish that Jesus be Jewish but not too Jewish.[15] More significantly, the question is important because its answer bears on the matter I'll take up in chapters 5 and 6, namely, what it was that Jesus intended his disciples to be praying for when they recited the prayer he gave them? For if the substance and language of the Disciples' Prayer is by and large based on and derived from the Jewish prayers it resembles, then it seems reasonable to conclude that the intended aim of the Disciples' Prayer is more than likely the same as the aim of those prayers.

How we answer this question is essential in assessing the validity of a view of the nature and aim of the prayer that has been dominant in New Testament scholarship for more than one hundred years—namely, that the Disciples' Prayer is an "eschatological prayer."

---

15. A view that James H. Charlesworth notes is "a bewitching oxymoron" ("A Caveat on Textual Transmission and the Meaning of Abba: A Study of the Lord's Prayer," in *The Lord's Prayer and Other Prayer Texts from the Greco-Roman Era*, ed. James H. Charlesworth, Mark Harding, and Mark Christopher Kiley [Valley Forge, PA: Trinity Press International, 1994], 5.

That is, to paraphrase Jeremias, the foremost proponent of this view, the prayer is wholeheartedly directed toward the achievement or manifestation of the "age of salvation" that Jews, including Jesus, believed was near at hand; thus Jesus is urging his disciples to "pray down" the expected gifts of this age "even here and even here, today."[16] The belief that the Disciples' Prayer is indeed derived from the Amidah, the Kaddish, and the Morning Prayer, twined with the view that these prayers are themselves "eschatological" in nature, is one of the major buttresses supporting this view of the prayer's nature.

In the face of a number of very prominent scholars who have said otherwise, I think the answer to the question is no: The Disciples' Prayer was *not* based on, let alone derived from the Kaddish, the Amidah, or the Morning Prayer. Despite claims to the contrary, we have no real evidence that these prayers actually existed, let alone were used by Palestinian Jews, in the first half of the first century CE, at least in the form and wording that those who argue for this view assume they had. Nor do we have any strong reason to believe that Jesus would have known them if they were so used and had the form Jeremias attributes to them early in the first century CE.

It should be noted, and noted well, that our earliest testimony to the Kaddish as a prescribed daily prayer appears in a tractate of the Babylonian Talmud that dates to the sixth century CE. As Jewish experts on first-century Jewish prayer such as Solomon Zeitlin,[17] Ezra Fleischer,[18] Lee Levine,[19] Stefan Reif,[20] and Paul F. Bradshaw[21] have

---

16. Joachim Jeremias, *The Lord's Prayer* (Philadelphia: Fortress Press, 1964), 27.
17. Solomon Zeitlin, "The Tefillah, the Shemoneh Esreh: An Historical Study of the First Canonization of the Hebrew Liturgy," *Jewish Quarterly Review* n.s. 54 (1964): 208–49.
18. Ezra Fleischer, "On the Beginnings of Obligatory Jewish Prayer," *Tarbiz* 59 (1990): 397–425 (in Hebrew; English summary, iii–v); Fleischer, "The Shemone Esre—Its Character, Internal Order, Contents and Goals," *Tarbiz* 62 (1993): 179–223 (in Hebrew; English summary, vi–vii).
19. Lee Levine, "The Second Temple Synagogue: The Formative Years," in *The Synagogue in Late Antiquity*, ed. Lee Levine (Philadelphia: ASOR, 1987), 14–19.

noted, the Amidah, let alone the form of the Amidah that contains the words "Restore our judges as at first and our counselors as in the beginning, and you yourself reign over us" and the petition for forgiveness, does not seem to have come into being until after the fall of the temple in 70 CE, an event that was more likely than not the impetus for its creation. The Kaddish as we know it does not seem to have appeared until post-talmudic times. And the Morning Prayer that Jeremias and others hold to be the background to the "temptation" clause in the Disciples' Prayer appears to have been composed and in circulation no earlier than the third century of our era.[22]

But even if each of these prayers is "early"—that is, in the first half of the first century CE—should we conclude that Jesus would have known them? Many students of the Disciples' Prayer have said yes. After all, the Kaddish and the Amidah (but not the Morning Prayer) were, they declare, synagogue prayers—that is, prayers whose "home" was the institution in which, from their early youth on, Jews, including Jesus, were schooled and disciplined in the practice of prayer. Moreover, these prayers were, they argue or assume, a vital part of the worship services that were regularly conducted in the synagogue. I. Howard Marshall speaks for many when he claims that

> After private prayer on entry to the building by the worshippers there was a public confession of the Jewish faith in the Shema (Dt. 6:4-9;

---

20. Stefan C. Reif, *Judaism and Hebrew Prayer* (Cambridge: Cambridge University Press, 1993), 44–52, 82–87.
21. Paul F. Bradshaw, "Jewish Influence on Early Christian Liturgy: A Reappraisal," *Jewish-Christian Relations*, January 7, 2008, http://www.jcrelations.net/Jewish_Influence_on_Early_Christian_Liturgy__A_Reappraisal.3217.0.html.
22. For concise discussion of these matters, see Crump, *Knocking on Heaven's Door*, 107–12; and Richard Wendel, "Appendix E: The Problem of Associating the Lord's Prayer with Jewish Statutory Prayers," in "The Interpretation of the Lord's Prayer, Q 11:2b-4, in the Formative Stratum of Q According to the Literary and Cultural Perspectives Afforded by the Affixed Aphorisms, Q 11:9-10, 11-13" (PhD diss., Loyola University, 2010), 265–71, http://ecommons.luc.edu/cgi/viewcontent.cgi?article=1078&context=luc_diss.

THE DISCIPLES' PRAYER

11:13-21), followed by prayers, including the Tephillah and the Shemoneh Esreh. Then came the centre of the worship, the reading of the Scriptures. A passage from the Pentateuch was read, according to a fixed scheme of lections, by several members of the congregation in turn, with an Aramaic paraphrase. There was also a lesson from the prophets.... It is safest to assume that there was at least some freedom of choice of prophetic reading in the first century. Following the readings was a prayer, and then came a sermon, if there was somebody competent present to give one (Acts 13:15). Finally the Qaddish prayer was recited. The readers for the day were appointed before the service began.[23]

So, the argument goes, how could Jesus not have known these prayers? Indeed, if we work from what we know about our how *our* sense of the forms and aims and language proper to prayer comes about—through "sacred association" of hearing particular prayers uttered in churches and synagogues and other places of worship in which believers have been raised—these prayers would have been the very font and ground of his understanding both of the forms and language in which prayer should be uttered, as well as of the concerns and foci that prayer should have.

But this view is extremely problematic. In the first place, even should we grant for the sake of argument that these prayers existed in the first century, we have no evidence in any Jewish source that the Amidah and the Kaddish were regularly, let alone prescribed to be, communally recited in the synagogue. For it is now clear, thanks to the investigations of Lee Levine and Richard Horsley on

---

23. I. Howard Marshall, *The Gospel of Luke: A Commentary on the Greek Text*, New International Greek Testament Commentary (Grand Rapids: Eerdmans, 1978), 181. The "many" include, but are not limited to, Jeremias ("Daily Prayer in the Life of Jesus and the Primitive Church," in *The Prayers of Jesus* [London: SCM, 1967], 66–78), Paul Billerbeck ("Ein Synagogengottesdienst in Jesu Tagen," ZNW 55 [1965], 143–61), E. Schürer (*The History of the Jewish People in the Age of Jesus Christ*, ed. Geza Vermes, Fergus Millar, and Matthew Black [Edinburgh: T&T Clark, 1973–1987], 2:423–63, esp. 447–63), Darrell Bock (*The Gospel of Luke* [Grand Rapids, Baker, 1994], 1:401), John Nolland (*Luke 9:21—18:34*, Word Biblical Commentary [Dallas: Word, 1993]. 193), Joseph A. Fitzmyer (*The Gospel according to Luke*, AB [New York: Doubleday, 1985], 531), and H. Schürmann (*Das Lukasevangelium* [Freiburg: Herder, 1969], 1:228–29]).

first-century-CE synagogues, and of E. P. Sanders on the beliefs and practices of Palestinian (or Formative) Judaism, that there was no fixed synagogue liturgy in Palestinian synagogues until at least well into the second century of our era. Moreover, they further point out that first-century Palestinian synagogues were not places of communal prayer.[24] They were instead places dedicated only to Torah recitation and instruction.[25]

Nor do early Christian sources give any warrant for seeing communal prayer as taking place in synagogues. In fact, in each of the New Testament references to synagogues and the activities going on in them, there is never any mention of prayer of *any* kind, let alone prayer in unison or public recitation of the Amidah or the Kaddish. What *is* mentioned, however, as going on there is Torah reading, explication, and instruction. Moreover, in every story in the New Testament that speaks of Jesus going into, or being in, a synagogue, there is never any description of an intent on his part to pray when he gets there, or of his actually doing so, let alone praying with others. What he is presented as going into a synagogue to do, as well as actually doing while he is there, is to read Torah, to engage in teaching, or to argue with others about things related to the Jewish law (see Mark 1:21-28; 6:1-2; Luke 4:15, 16-30).

This is not to say that no first-century Jews prayed in or at synagogues. Josephus tells us otherwise.[26] But as he—and a host of other sources—note, any prayer that was uttered there was always private and spontaneous and was never, unless by accident, precisely

---

24. Lee Levine, *The Ancient Synagogue: The First Thousand Years*, 2nd ed. (New Haven: Yale University Press, 2005), 162–69; Richard A. Horsley, *Galilee: History, Politics, People* (Valley Forge, PA: Trinity Press International, 1995), 225; E. P. Sanders, *Judaism: Practice and Belief, 63 BCE–66 CE* (London: SCM, 1992), 198–200.
25. On this, see Levine, *The Ancient Synagogue*, 155–57; Sanders, *Judaism*, 199–200.
26. Josephus, *Life* 294–295.

the same prayer anyone else might have been praying at the same time, let alone something intentionally said in unison with others.[27]

In the second place, the view that Jesus must have known these prayers is based on a hidden, and question-begging, but nevertheless widely held and (so far as I can see) unquestioned assumption, namely, that Jesus grew up going to, and under the influence of, the synagogue. But this assumption overlooks the fact that we have no positive evidence that Jesus actually did so. The closest we come to this is Luke 4:16: "And he came to Nazareth, where he had been brought up; and he went to the synagogue, as his custom was, on the Sabbath day" (NRSV). But this text will not bear the evidentiary weight placed on it. The statement above is part of the larger story, in Luke 4:17-30, of how Jesus was rejected by his own people and expelled from their synagogue for declaring apodictically that the divine plan for the liberation of the oppressed spoken of in Isaiah 61 had "today" been inaugurated with God's selection of Jesus as its agent, and that it did not, contrary to expectations, involve vengeance against the enemies of Israel. In any case, this story is probably not historical.[28] More importantly, even if we assume that Luke 4:16-30 is an authentic record of an actual historical event, all that may be legitimately inferred is that Jesus made it his practice to go into the synagogue when he was an adult, not when he was a boy.

It is extremely difficult to think that Jesus could have matured in a synagogue environment since, as many scholars have argued, so far as we know from both archaeology and literary sources, neither

---

27. Sanders, *Judaism*, 207–8.
28. Luke's story is usually regarded as his wholesale reworking for his own theological purposes of Mark 6:1-6. On this, See John Nolland, *Luke 1:1—9:20*, Word Biblical Commentary (Dallas: Word, 1989), 192–93. See, too, E. Haenchen, "Historie und Verkündigung bei Markus und Lukas," in *Das Lukas-Evangelium. Die redaktions- und kompositionsgeschichtliche Forschung*, ed. Georg Braumann, Wege der Forschung 280 (Darmstadt, Wissenschaftliche Buchgesellschaft, 1973), 287–316.

Jesus' home village of Nazareth nor any village in its proximity had a synagogue for anyone to grow up in.[29]

I note in passing that recently, my friend J. D. G. (Jimmy) Dunn, Emeritus Lightfoot Professor of Divinity in the Department of Theology at the University of Durham, has attempted in his article "Did Jesus Attend the Synagogue?"[30] to mitigate the fact, which he himself acknowledges, that there is no archaeological evidence of a first-century synagogue at Nazareth. He does this by noting that "very little archaeological investigation has been possible" at sites in Nazareth where a synagogue might have stood, since, "unlike Capernaum" (where there is evidence for a synagogue, albeit a second- or third-century one), "later and modern buildings obscure the site." But to my eyes, this attempt is essentially an appeal to the questionable principle that "the absence of evidence is not evidence of absence." Dunn's argument is itself mitigated not only by the fact that we have no archaeological evidence for the existence of first-century synagogues in *any* pre-70 Jewish village in Galilee save perhaps for Tiberias, Capernaum, and Magdala but also by Josephus's notice that the only synagogues that did exist in Galilee prior to the war were those at Dora (*Ant.* 19.6.3), Tiberias (*Life* 54), and Caesarea (*Jewish War* 2.14–4.5).

So even if pre-second-century Palestinian synagogues were places of communal prayer, let alone places of communal prayer that followed a fixed liturgy in which the Kaddish and the Amidah played

---

29. On this, see Mark A. Chancey (*The Myth of a Gentile Galilee: The Population of Galilee and New Testament Studies* [Cambridge: Cambridge University Press, 2002], 66); Z. Ilan ("Galilee: Survey of Synagogues," *Excavations and Surveys in Israel* 5 [1986–1987]: 35–37); P. V. McCracken Flesher ("Palestinian Synagogues before 70 C.E.: A Review of the Evidence," in *Ancient Synagogues: Historical Analysis and Archaeological Discovery*, ed. D. Urman and P. V. McCracken Flesher [Leiden: Brill, 1995], 1:27–39).
30. The article is found in *Jesus and Archaeology*, James Charlesworth, ed. [Grand Rapids: Eerdmans, 2006]).

a part, we still need not—and in my eyes should not—conclude that Jesus would have known these prayers.

Finally, the formal and linguistic parallels that many see as existing between the Disciples' Prayer and these three prayers, or at least between the Disciples' Prayer and the Amidah and the Kaddish, are, I think, far more apparent than real. In fact, it looks to me as if the perception of strong parallels between these prayers involves both reading things into the Disciples' Prayer that aren't there and ignoring radical formal and linguistic differences between them. For example, the notion that the Disciples' Prayer and the Amidah share the same form is grounded in two questionable assumptions: (1) that the tripartite structure exhibited in the Amidah was unique to it and not typical of Jewish prayer in general, and (b) that, contrary to what we have seen is actually the case (cf. above, pp. 12–14), the Disciples' Prayer originally concluded with a doxology.

In order to say that the "name," "kingdom," and "forgiveness" clauses of the Disciples' Prayer are derived from, or directly influenced, respectively by the "name" request in the Kaddish, the "kingdom" requests in the Kaddish and the Amidah, and the "forgiveness" request in the Amidah, one must explain away or overlook two facts. First, the "name," "kingdom," and "forgiveness" requests in the Disciples' Prayer do not actually comport formally or stylistically with their alleged counterparts. They are, in terms of length, far shorter. They are not set out in the multiline structure in which their alleged counterparts are cast. Nor do they contain anything like the benedictions with which these alleged counterparts are capped. Moreover, in the "name" and "kingdom" requests in the Disciples' Prayer, God is addressed in the second person, but in the Kaddish (as well as in what came to be statutory synagogal prayers) God is spoken of in the third person.

Second, there is a significant linguistic difference between the "kingdom" clause in the Disciples' Prayer and the "kingdom" clauses in the Kaddish and the Amidah. The verb used in the first case is the verb "to come" (ἐλθέτω [*elthetō*], a third-person imperative form, used impersonally, of ἔρχεσθαι [*erchesthai*], "to come"). But in the Kaddish and the Amidah, the formulations used with reference to God's kingdom are, first, a petition in the third person using the verb "establish" or "make manifest"—"May He establish His kingdom"—and in the second, a second-person imperative of the verb "to reign": "You yourself reign over us, you alone." Moreover, the verb "come" is not used in coordination with the noun "kingdom," in Greek or Hebrew or Aramaic, in Jewish literature of this period (except for a single exception of Mic. 4:8), and thus the construction in the Disciples' Prayer can hardly be regarded as typical of Jewish prayers in this period.[31]

In the light of these considerations, does it really seem likely that the Disciples' Prayer was based on and derived from the Kaddish and the Amidah? Shouldn't we have expected to see far more formal, stylistic, and linguistic conformity between them if this was indeed the case? The expectation seems valid since, as Heineman has noted in his examination of the background of the Disciples' Prayer, the tendency when one was basing a new prayer on one that was already rooted in liturgy was not just to allude in one way or another to the existing prayer or prayers, but to take up intact the exact wording of phrases, even whole sentences, from the exemplar.[32] On these grounds, the derivation of the Disciples' Prayer from the named Jewish prayers is not likely.

---

31. The construction in Mic. 4:8 is the imperfect in Hebrew, *ûbō'â*, and the future indicative in Greek, "shall come" (εἰσελεύσεται [*eiseleusetai*]); neither offers a parallel to the third-person aorist imperative used in the Disciples' Prayer.
32. See Joseph Heineman, "The Background of Jesus' Prayer" in Petuchowski and Brocke, *The Lord's Prayer and the Jewish Liturgy*, 88.

THE DISCIPLES' PRAYER

But what makes it certain that the Disciples' Prayer was not based on and derived from the Kaddish and the Amidah, or any purportedly early Jewish communal prayer, is not what appears there, but what does not. There is no appeal to the patriarchs, no mention of Israel, no nationalistic cast to the petitions, and no concrete depiction of any future hope, as there is in the Kaddish and especially the Amidah.

At this point, we have established three things about the Disciples' Prayer. It is most certainly a prayer and not a compendium of Christian doctrine. It is a Jewish prayer. And, from all appearances, it is the creation of a particular individual, not simply a derivative from corporate prayers allegedly (but doubtfully) used in synagogue worship in the first century. But who was that individual? And who, in his eyes, were those whom he intended to pray the prayer he created? These are extremely important questions. As will be seen below, the answers we give to them are vital to helping us reach the primary goal of this book, determining so far as we are able the original meaning of the Disciples' Prayer.

4

The Prayer's Author and His Disciples

In previous chapters I have argued, against Michael Goulder, John Dominic Crossan, and others, that the "author" of the Disciples' Prayer in its balanced Matthean form was indeed Jesus of Nazareth.[1] But who was Jesus?

The Author of the Disciples' Prayer

This simple question is often quickly answered. "He was the Messiah" or "the Son of God" or "He was humanity's Savior." For my purposes,

---

1. So also Hans Dieter Betz, *The Sermon on the Mount: A Commentary on the Sermon on the Mount, Including the Sermon on the Plain (Matthew 5:3—7:27 and Luke 6:20-49)*, ed. Adela Yarbro Collins, Hermeneia (Minneapolis: Fortress Press, 1995), 372. And it is quite clear when one surveys the literature on the Disciples' Prayer that the majority of scholars who have dealt with this question of whether Matthew and Luke and the Didache are correct in noting that the prayer actually originates with Jesus have followed ancient tradition and answered in the affirmative, even if they think that what is presented within Matthew and Luke and the Didache is in form and wording an expansion, a recasting, or a compilation of words that Jesus spoke to his disciples. But it should be noted that a small number of exegetes claim that the actual "author" of the prayer was not Jesus, but the prophetic figure with whom Jesus initially associated himself before embarking on his own ministry, John the Baptizer. For an assessment of this view, see the appendix below.

THE DISCIPLES' PRAYER

these answers, and others like them, are of little help historically, being in the end essentially faith-based evaluations of Jesus' significance, which are incapable of historical confirmation. The historical question about Jesus is more to my point, but it is not a simple one to answer. The primary sources we have at our disposal for answering it—the Gospels of Matthew, Mark, Luke, and John—do not easily lend themselves to our doing so. As Gospel criticism over the last one hundred years has shown, they are neither objective histories nor biographies in any modern sense of the word. Nor, despite demurrals within them to the contrary (such as Luke 1:1-4), are they primarily concerned with presenting facts about Jesus' life and teaching, let alone getting the facts of Jesus' life and teaching "right." For, as a glance at the scholarly tool known as a Gospel synopsis shows, they not only contradict one another but do so as much, if not more frequently, than they agree with each other.[2] The Gospels are, rather, interpretations and presentations in narrative form of the significance of their central subject.[3] Their presentations are set within a larger framework whose center is the Jewish story of how the God of Israel acts to fulfill his promises to his covenant

---

2. Consider, for instance, the story of Jesus on the cross, which is found in all four Gospels (Matt. 27:33-56 // Mark 15:37-41 // Luke 23:32-49 // John 19:17-37). Mark presents Jesus as dying totally abandoned and alone—all of his followers save for some women who are said to be standing far off have fled and both of the two men who are crucified at his side revile him—and, save for his recitation of a portion of Psalm 21, as remaining silent when people mock him. In Luke's version of these events, Jesus speaks words of forgiveness to those who excoriate him, and one of those who is crucified with him pronounces him innocent of any crime. In John's version of the event, which takes place on a day quite different from when Matthew, Mark, and Luke tell us it occurred, we have Jesus' mother and a disciple at the foot of the cross where they are blessed by Jesus with words that cannot be found anywhere in the Synoptic records of the events. Luke places Jesus' rejection at the synagogue in his hometown of Nazareth as one of the first events of his public ministry (Luke 4:16-30). However, Mark places it much later, about halfway through his Galilean ministry (Mark 6:1-6). Mark places Jesus' calling of the disciples before his Capernaum preaching (Mark 1:16-20), while Luke places it after (Luke 5:1-11). In John, Jesus does not perform exorcisms or speak in aphorisms and parables, as he does in Matthew, Mark, and Luke. Other examples could be multiplied.
3. For a popular exposition and defense of this view of the Gospels, see Richard A. Burridge, *Four Gospels, One Jesus? A Symbolic Reading*, 2nd ed. (London: SPCK, 2005).

people and is bringing them to the destiny he has appointed for them, as the nation that will bring blessings to all the peoples of the earth.[4]

I nevertheless believe, despite all the difficulties our sources pose for answering our question, that there are still several facts about Jesus we can hold with reasonable certainty.

- He was a first-century Palestinian Jew. This means that his worldview would have been grounded in and shaped by certain fundamental beliefs held by other Palestinian Jews: that Yahweh, the God of Israel, alone was god; that Yahweh had created the universe for the benefit of humankind and intended it to be a place where peace and justice prevailed; that Yahweh had chosen Israel to be his instrument through which he would accomplish his purposes for the world; and, to quote Tom Wright, "that [Yahweh] would act for [Israel] and through her [would] re-establish his judgment and his justice, his wisdom and his Shalom, throughout the world" when Israel was oppressed by forces that refused to recognize that Yahweh was Lord.[5]

- Jesus was vitally concerned with questions of what might be called national policy, for example: What does it mean to be the nation chosen of God to bring blessing and a knowledge of the one true creator God to all peoples, and had his own perception, which he believed to be divinely authorized, of how Israel could and should preserve its character and its mission to be a nation of priests in a world overrun by pagans and their sympathizers.[6]

- He was convinced that the way many of his fellow Jews had

---

4. On this, see N. T. Wright, *The New Testament and the People of God*, Christian Origins and the Question of God 1 (Minneapolis: Fortress Press, 1992), 279.
5. Wright, *The New Testament and the People of God*, 279.
6. G.B. Caird, *Jesus and the Jewish Nation* (London: Athlone, 1965), http://www.biblicalstudies.org.uk/pdf/emwl/jesus_caird.pdf); Caird, *New Testament Theology* (Oxford: Clarendon Press, 1994), 356–58.

been answering this question was bringing Israel to the verge of a national calamity.[7]

- He viewed himself, and was viewed by others, as appointed and empowered by God as first and foremost a prophet to Israel, who had been given an urgent mission to call God's people, through word and deed, away from the particular ways of being Israel that those whom he addressed were pursuing and toward an alternative vision of what faithfulness to the God of Israel entailed.[8] This vision involved the rejection of the idea, held by many in his day and afterward, that God calls for revolutionary and retaliatory violence against those whom certain of his coreligionists viewed as the enemies of Israel.[9]

- He called and gathered to himself a select group of disciples to "be with him" and to follow him. He instructed them more intensively than any other group he addressed, both in what it would entail for them to remain true in their words and deeds to his vision of faithfulness to the God of Israel, and in the vital necessity for them to do so.

Granting all of this, other questions now need to be answered if we are to understand what the words of the Disciples' Prayer meant to Jesus. The first is: Why did Jesus call disciples? Why did he feel, as he evidently did, that it was necessary to have them? And why did he give them the prayer he did? What prompted him to do so? To answer these questions, we first need to establish just who Jesus

---

7. Caird, *New Testament Theology*, 361–66.
8. On this, see R. David Kaylor, *Jesus the Prophet: His Vision of the Kingdom on Earth* (Louisville: Westminster John Knox, 1994); Edward P. Meadors, *Jesus the Messianic Herald of Salvation* (Tübingen: Mohr Siebeck, 1995); N. T. Wright, *Jesus and the Victory of God*, Christian Origins and the Question of God 2 (Minneapolis: Fortress Press, 1996), 147–97.
9. Scot McKnight, *A New Vision for Israel: The Teachings of Jesus in National Context* (Grand Rapids: Eerdmans, 1999); Richard Horsley, *The Prophet Jesus and the Renewal of Israel: Moving Beyond a Diversionary Debate* (Grand Rapids: Eerdmans, 2012).

assumed his disciples as a group to be when he urged the Disciples' Prayer on them.

The Recipients of the Disciples' Prayer

It is quite clear from the Gospels that the ones to whom Jesus gives the Disciples' Prayer are at the very least, like Jesus, Jews. They are also among those to whom Jesus has addressed a programmatic and urgent call to "turn" in obedience to the ways of God, which he proclaims are now more than ever incumbent upon those who would be God's people (see Matt. 4:17; Luke 4:16-23). But, more importantly, the disciples are those, among all the other groups whom Jesus addresses with this call, whom Jesus specifically chose to become υἱοὶ θεοῦ (*huioi theou*), "sons of God."[10] They were the faithful remnant of Israel that, among other things, was to hallow God's name and bring knowledge of him to the world (Matt. 5:11, 13-14; Luke 6:12-16, 22-23) by conforming their lives to what Jesus taught them to see was the pattern of faithfulness that such υἱοί owe their Father. This pattern was rooted squarely in an understanding of God as the supremely caring Father who can be relied on implicitly to know and provide for all of his children's needs. This pattern consequently constrains υἱοὶ θεοῦ to trust in that care even—indeed, especially—when evidence of it seems sorely lacking and God seems to have abandoned them.[11] And what was this pattern? What did

---

10. On this see, e.g., Jack Dean Kingsbury, *Jesus Christ in Matthew, Mark, and Luke* (Philadelphia: Fortress Press, 1981), 20; H. Windisch, "Friedensbringer—Gottessöhne: Eine religionsgeschichtliche Interpretation der 7. Seligpreisung," *Zeitschrift für die neutestamentliche Wissenschaft und die Kunde der älteren Kirche* 24 (1925): 240-60; Eduard Schweizer, υἱός, υἱοθεσία, in *Theological Dictionary of the New Testament*, ed. Gerhard Kittel and Gerhard Friedrich, trans. Geoffrey W. Bromiley, 10 vols. [hereafter *TDNT*] (Grand Rapids: Eerdmans, 1964–1976), 8:389.
11. John S. Kloppenborg, *The Formation of Q: Trajectories in Ancient Wisdom Collections* (Augsburg Fortress, 1987) 241; Kloppenborg, "The Sayings Gospel Q and the Quest for the Historical Jesus," *HTR* 89 (1996): 330.

THE DISCIPLES' PRAYER

Jesus teach them in this regard? How, according to Jesus, was their filial obligation to flesh itself out?

To answer this, let's first note two things about Jesus' teaching on discipleship. First, it takes its cue from the presentation in the book of Deuteronomy regarding (a) who Israel was divinely commissioned to be and (b) what faithful Israelites were exhorted to do to avoid showing themselves as a "wicked and adulterous generation." This notably involved, among other things, not grumbling against God when he provided for their needs, not doubting the efficacy of his ways for them to bring them to their promised its destiny, and not putting him to the test.[12] This fact will prove to be significant when we come below to assess the long-standing and widespread view that the aim of the Disciples' Prayer is to pray down into the present some things that Jews thought to belong properly to Israel's expected future.

The second thing to note is that Jesus' teaching on the nature of discipleship is formulated both positively (Matt. 6:25–34 // Luke 12:22–31) and negatively (e.g., Mark 10:42). In the latter case, it's often phrased in terms of not being like those whom Jesus calls the "hypocrites." His disciples are not to think or act like their coreligionists who, according to Jesus, have taken on the mantle of their faithless ancestors who were known in his time as "that generation"—the generation that, after the exodus, in the wilderness, at Massah and Meribah, had "hardened their hearts," erred, and tested and put God to the proof. Though they had seen his work for them,

---

12. This, notably, is also what is set out by all three Synoptic evangelists in their programmatic and ministry-prefacing stories of Jesus' "temptation" in the wilderness (Mark 1:1:12-13 // Matt. 4:1-11 // Luke 4:1-13) in which Jesus is explicitly tested as the Deuteronomic "son"/Israel who must not grumble against God, doubt the efficacy of God's ways, or put God to the test. On this, see my *The Temptations of Jesus in Early Christianity* (Sheffield: Sheffield Academic Press, 1995), 85–87.

that generation had refused to "regard" his ways, and thus were prevented from entering God's promised "rest" (see Psalm 95).

Jesus taught a number of things about how one becomes or remains a "son" of God. Some of them involved eschewing traditional sources of gaining or maintaining "honor," such as family connections (see Matt. 10:37-38 // Luke 14:25-35; Matt. 12:46-50 // 8:19-21 // Mark 3:31-35), wealth (Matt. 19:23 // Mark 10:17–23 // Luke 18:24), social status (Matt. 18:1-5 // Mark 9:33-37 // Luke 9:46-48), and possessions (Matt. 19:16–30 // Mark 10:17–31 // Luke 18:18–30). But it seems that the most important of these ways had to do what Jesus called "taking up his cross," "denying oneself," "manifesting true greatness," showing indiscriminate and limitless forgiveness (especially of one's enemies), and being what Jesus called an εἰρηνοποιός (*eirēnopoios*), a "peacemaker."

Let's be clear on what these five things entail by looking at the texts in which Jesus' teaching on cross-bearing, self-denial, true greatness, forgiveness, and being a peacemaker appear.

Cross-Bearing and Self Denial

We find Jesus' teaching on cross-bearing and self-denial in two places in the Synoptic Gospels—Matt. 10:37-39 // Luke 14:26-27 (see table 4.1) and Matt. 16:13-27; Mark 8:27–30; Luke 9:18-27 (see table 4.2)—and in an agraphon in the Gospel of Thomas.[13]

---

13. "Whoever will not take up his cross as I do, will not be worthy of me" (Gospel of Thomas 55).

THE DISCIPLES' PRAYER

Matt. 10:37-39 // Luke 14:26-27

Whoever loves father or mother more than me is not worthy of me; and whoever loves son or daughter more than me is not worthy of me; and whoever does not take up the cross and follow me is not worthy of me. Those who find their life will lose it, and those who lose their life for my sake will find it.	Whoever comes to me and does not hate father and mother, wife and children, brothers and sisters, yes, and even life itself, cannot be my disciple. Whoever does not carry the cross and follow me cannot be my disciple.

Table 4.1

Matt. 16:13–27; Mark 8:27–30; Luke 9:18-27

Now when Jesus came into the district of Caesarea Philippi, he asked his disciples, "Who do people say that the Son of Man is?" And they said, "Some say John the Baptist, but others Elijah, and still others Jeremiah or one of the prophets." He said to them, "But who do you say that I am?" Simon Peter answered, "You are the Messiah, the Son of the living God." . . .	Jesus went on with his disciples to the villages of Caesarea Philippi; and on the way he asked his disciples, "Who do people say that I am?" And they answered him, "John the Baptist; and others, Elijah; and still others, one of the prophets." He asked them, "But who do you say that I am?" Peter answered him, "You are the Messiah."	Once when Jesus was praying alone, with only the disciples near him, he asked them, "Who do the crowds say that I am?" They answered, "John the Baptist; but others, Elijah; and still others, that one of the ancient prophets has arisen." He said to them, "But who do you say that I am?" Peter answered, "The Messiah of God."
Then he sternly ordered the disciples not to tell anyone that he was the Messiah.	And he sternly ordered them not to tell anyone about him.	He sternly ordered and commanded them not to tell anyone,
From that time on, Jesus began to show his disciples that he must go to Jerusalem and undergo great suffering at the hands of the elders and chief priests and scribes, and be killed, and on the third day be raised. And Peter took him aside and began to rebuke him, saying, "God forbid it, Lord! This must never happen to you."	Then he began to teach them that the Son of Man must undergo great suffering, and be rejected by the elders, the chief priests, and the scribes, and be killed, and after three days rise again. He said all this quite openly. And Peter took him aside and began to rebuke him.	saying, "The Son of Man must undergo great suffering, and be rejected by the elders, chief priests, and scribes, and be killed, and on the third day be raised."

THE PRAYER'S AUTHOR AND HIS DISCIPLES

But he turned and said to Peter, "Get behind me, Satan! You are a stumbling block to me; for you are setting your mind not on divine things but on human things."	But turning and looking at his disciples, he rebuked Peter and said, "Get behind me, Satan! For you are setting your mind not on divine things but on human things."	
Then Jesus told his disciples,	He called the crowd with his disciples, and said to them,	Then he said to them all,
"If any want to become my followers, let them deny themselves and take up their cross and follow me. For those who want to save their life will lose it, and those who lose their life for my sake will find it.	"If any want to become my followers, let them deny themselves and take up their cross and follow me. For those who want to save their life will lose it, and those who lose their life for my sake, and for the sake of the gospel, will save it.	"If any want to become my followers, let them deny themselves and take up their cross daily and follow me. For those who want to save their life will lose it, and those who lose their life for my sake will save it.
For what will it profit them if they gain the whole world but forfeit their life? Or what will they give in return for their life?"	For what will it profit them to gain the whole world and forfeit their life? Indeed, what can they give in return for their life?"	What does it profit them if they gain the whole world, but lose or forfeit themselves?"

Table 4.2

These texts show that the disciples' cross is not what it is often thought to be—a metaphor for some difficult family situation, a personal loss, a crushing debt, the frustration of one's hopes, a nagging in-law. It is, rather, what Jesus' cross was—the price likely to be extracted by the rulers of the world for one's nonconformity to the ways of the world and for challenging injustice and worldly conceptions of power.[14] For this is not only what brought Jesus himself to be crucified. It was what he was consciously aware would bring him to this end. So being a "son of God" entails being ready

---

14. On this, see especially John Howard Yoder, *The Politics of Jesus*, 2nd ed. (Grand Rapids: Eerdmans, 1994), 95–96.

and willing to endure persecution and suffering, even to the point of martyrdom, for the sake of faithfulness to God (cf. e.g., Matt. 5:9-12).

Self-Denial

Despite what many of us who were brought up in penitential atmospheres have been taught, in the teaching of Jesus to "deny oneself" (ἀπαρνησάσθω ἑαυτῷ [*aparnēsasthō heautō*]), especially when it is linked, as it is here, with a command to "take up one's cross," has little to do with the practice of asceticism (i.e., to deny something, especially pleasures, to oneself). Rather, it involves the rejection of a presumed prerogative, in this case the right to defend one's life (ψυχὴν αὐτοῦ σῶσαι [*psychēn autou sōsai*]) at all costs when faced with danger or death. More particularly, when we take into account how Jesus links "saving" one's life with seeking "to gain the whole world" (κερδῆσαι τὸν κόσμον ὅλον [*kerdēsai ton kosmon holon*]) and what seeking "to gain the whole world" signifies, to "deny oneself" means to give up as valid any idea that one has the right to preserve self or life from danger or death through the exercise of self-aggrandizing power.[15] So, "to deny oneself" entails not only accepting a posture of defenselessness in the face of danger and death but also rejecting seeking worldly power and dominion through worldly means.

Servanthood as True Greatness

Jesus' teaching about "true greatness" is found at Matt. 18:1–5; Mark 9:33–35; and Luke 9:46–48 (see table 4.3).

---

15. In its abstract sense, κερδαίνω means simply "to procure gain, advantage, profit." But with κόσμος as its object, κερδαίνω means winning lordship over the world and gaining all the possibilities for self-aggrandizement that such lordship allows. See H. Schlier, "κερδος, κερδαίνω," *TDNT* 3:673.

THE PRAYER'S AUTHOR AND HIS DISCIPLES

Matt. 18:1–5; Mark 9:33-35; and Luke 9:46–48

At that time the disciples came to Jesus and asked, "Who is the greatest in the kingdom of heaven?" He called a child, whom he put among them, and said,	Then they came to Capernaum; and when he was in the house he asked them, "What were you arguing about on the way?" But they were silent, for on the way they had argued with one another who was the greatest.	An argument arose among them as to which one of them was the greatest. But Jesus, aware of their inner thoughts,
"Truly I tell you, unless you change and become like children, you will never enter the kingdom of heaven.		took a little child and put it by his side, and said to them,
Whoever becomes humble like this child is the greatest in the kingdom of heaven. Whoever welcomes one such child in my name welcomes me."	He sat down, called the twelve, and said to them, "Whoever wants to be first must be last of all and servant of all." Then he took a little child and put it among them; and taking it in his arms, he said to them,	
	"Whoever welcomes one such child in my name welcomes me, and whoever welcomes me welcomes not me but the one who sent me."	"Whoever welcomes this child in my name welcomes me, and whoever welcomes me welcomes the one who sent me; for the least among all of you is the greatest."

Table 4.3

It also appears at Matt. 20:26-27 // Mark 10:42-45, in a story of James and John (or their mother) asking for seats of honor next to Jesus when he is vindicated by God, and at Luke 22:24-27 in Luke's story of the Last Supper (see table 4.4). In order to understand what Jesus teaches his disciples about "true greatness" in these texts, it's important to be clear about why he speaks as he does.

THE DISCIPLES' PRAYER

Matt. 20:20-28 // Mark 10:35-45; Luke 22:14-27

Then the mother of the sons of Zebedee came to him with her sons, and kneeling before him, she asked a favor of him. And he said to her, "What do you want?"	James and John, the sons of Zebedee, came forward to him and said to him, "Teacher, we want you to do for us whatever we ask of you." And he said to them, "What is it you want me to do for you?"	When the hour came, he took his place at the table, and the apostles with him. He said to them, "I have eagerly desired to eat this Passover with you before I suffer; for I tell you, I will not eat it until it is fulfilled in the kingdom of God."
She said to him, "Declare that these two sons of mine will sit, one at your right hand and one at your left, in your kingdom."	And they said to him, "Grant us to sit, one at your right hand and one at your left, in your glory."	Then he took a cup, and after giving thanks he said, "Take this and divide it among yourselves; for I tell you that from now on I will not drink of the fruit of the vine until the kingdom of God comes."
But Jesus answered, "You do not know what you are asking. Are you able to drink the cup that I am about to drink?	But Jesus said to them, "You do not know what you are asking. Are you able to drink the cup that I drink, or be baptized with the baptism that I am baptized with?"	Then he took a loaf of bread, and when he had given thanks, he broke it and gave it to them, saying, "This is my body, which is given for you. Do this in remembrance of me."
They said to him, "We are able." He said to them, "You will indeed drink my cup,	They replied, "We are able." Then Jesus said to them, "The cup that I drink you will drink; and with the baptism with which I am baptized, you will be baptized;	And he did the same with the cup after supper, saying, "This cup that is poured out for you is the new covenant in my blood. But see, the one who betrays me is with me, and his hand is on the table.
but to sit at my right hand and at my left, this is not mine to grant, but it is for those for whom it has been prepared by my Father."	but to sit at my right hand or at my left is not mine to grant, but it is for those for whom it has been prepared."	For the Son of Man is going as it has been determined, but woe to that one by whom he is betrayed!" Then they began to ask one another which one of them it could be who would do this.
When the ten heard it, they were angry with the two brothers. But Jesus called them to him and said,	When the ten heard this, they began to be angry with James and John. So Jesus called them and said to them,	A dispute also arose among them as to which one of them was to be regarded as the greatest.

"You know that the rulers of the Gentiles lord it over them, and their great ones are tyrants over them.	"You know that among the Gentiles those whom they recognize as their rulers lord it over them, and their great ones are tyrants over them.	But he said to them, "The kings of the Gentiles lord it over them; and those in authority over them are called benefactors.
It will not be so among you; but whoever wishes to be great among you must be your servant, and whoever wishes to be first among you must be your slave;	But it is not so among you; but whoever wishes to become great among you must be your servant, and whoever wishes to be first among you must be slave of all.	But not so with you; rather the greatest among you must become like the youngest, and the leader like one who serves.
just as the Son of Man came not to be served but to serve, and to give his life a ransom for many."	For the Son of Man came not to be served but to serve, and to give his life a ransom for many."	For who is greater, the one who is at the table or the one who serves? Is it not the one at the table? But I am among you as one who serves."

Table 4.4

In the first set of texts, it is because, despite Jesus' explicit teaching at Caesarea Philippi on cross-bearing and self-denial (see above), the disciples have persisted in their wholesale misunderstanding of who they are and what they think they have a right to as disciples of one who they have come to believe is the Messiah of Israel and the "Son of Man." They apparently understand that identity in terms of who others ("men") think the Messiah is, namely, a warrior king. They also apparently identify Jesus with the figure whom Daniel called "the Son of Man," and described as having been "given dominion, and glory, and kingdom, that all peoples, and nations, and languages should serve him" (Dan. 7:14). First Enoch describes the Son of Man as authorized by God himself to rout "the kings and the mighty from their seats (and the strong from their thrones)," by

loosening the reigns of the strong
and breaking the teeth of the sinners
because they do not extol and praise him
nor humbly acknowledge whence the kingdom was
bestowed upon them. (1 Enoch 46:4-5; cf. 69:27)

Being made by God to sit "on the throne of his glory," this figure was commissioned to cause sinners (i.e., gentile oppressors and unfaithful Israelites) "to pass away and be destroyed from off the face of the earth"; he takes, rather than ransoms, the lives of his enemies.[16] Notably, this Son of Man also does not give up his life, let alone in the service of anyone, but instead is bestowed with a "dominion [ἐξουσία (*exousia*)] over others which shall not pass away, a kingdom [βασιλέια (*basileia*)] that shall not be destroyed" (Dan. 7:14, LXX). And with "the sum of judgment" (1 Enoch 69:27), that is, the right to, he will extract divine vengeance upon Israel's enemies.[17]

Presuming themselves to be "great," given their relationship with *this* Jesus, the disciples have been raising questions about who (among them) is "greatest." Clearly, they give vent to an understanding of "greatness" as meaning "first" (both as "best regarded" and as "highly privileged") and as something that, if possessed, would entitle them to disregard attending to those beneath them socially, especially those whom their culture has designated as ἔσχατοι, "last," i.e., διάκονοι = "servants/slaves" and παιδία = "children," those who were without status or rights and who therefore were expected to subject themselves to others.[18] But, as Jesus takes pains to tell them, they've got it all wrong. Greatness consists in being like a παιδίον, a helpless one,[19] and in humbly "receiving," "welcoming," and approving, not

---

16. C. K. Barrett, "The Background of Mark 10:45," in *New Testament Essays: Studies in Memory of Thomas Walter Manson*, ed. A. J. B. Higgins (Manchester: Manchester University Press, 1959), 1–18, esp. 9.
17. Morna Hooker, *The Son of Man in Mark* (London: SPCK, 1967), 141.
18. G. Kittle, "ἔσχατος," *TDNT* 2:698; H. W. Beyer, "διακονέω," *TDNT* 2:88.

despising or dominating, those without status, those whom one might ordinarily regard as undeserving of grace and service, and as contemptible.[20]

In the second set of texts, Jesus teaches on "true greatness" because the disciples are (again!) displaying another false understanding of what they can expect for themselves in the future given that they are disciples of Messiah Jesus, the Son of Man. As Matthew and Mark tell us, this is both "seats" εἷς σου ἐκ δεξιῶν καὶ εἷς ἐξ ἀριστερῶν (*heis sou ek dexiōn kai heis ex aristerōn*), at Jesus "right and left hand"—that is to say, places of honor next to a king[21]—as well as some kind of attendant worldly dominion when Jesus comes, as they are expecting he will, into sovereignty. Jesus responds to the request in three ways. First, he declares that the disciples do not "know" what they are asking (Οὐκ οἴδατε τί αἰτεῖσθε [*Ouk oidate ti aiteisthe*]); second, he holds up how the great ones of the gentiles (most certainly, at the very least, Roman emperors and their representatives) treat those under them as a counterexample of how, if they *are* to be great, the disciples must conduct themselves as the emissaries of the Son of Man; and third, he tells them what the divine mission of the Son of Man actually is.

Now, in denying that the disciples know what they are asking when they request the seats next to him, not only is Jesus making a statement of fact, but the scene also allows the Gospel writers to make an allusive juxtaposition in the course of their narrative. First, sitting

---

19. See the extended discussion of the Markan use of the term παιδίον in A. Ambrozic, *The Hidden Kingdom* (Washington, DC: Catholic Biblical Association, 1972) 148–58, where Ambrozic concludes that in Mark a παιδίον is "one who is last of all and expected to subject himself to others."
20. C. Clifton Black, *Mark* (Nashville: Abingdon, 2011), 215–16. On the meaning of the verb δέχομαι (*dechomai*) in Jesus' charge to the disciples to "welcome" παιδία "in his name," see W. Grundmann, δέχομαι, *TDNT* 2:50–54.
21. See 1 Kgs. 2:19; 1 Esdras 4:29; Eccl. 12:12; Josephus, *Antiquities of the Jews* 6.11.9, where the seats on the right and on the left are royal stations.

THE DISCIPLES' PRAYER

at his "right and left hand" actually entails the opposite of what the disciples envisage this to be.[22] Second, if the disciples knew this, they would not be so eager to have their request granted them, let alone to make it. For as both Matt. 27:38 and Mark 15:27 show, to be "on the right and on the left" of Jesus is to occupy not positions of power but a place in the shadow of the cross, for there it is recorded that those who are granted to be at the respective sides of Jesus, and notably, at the very point at which Jesus is publicly proclaimed to be King of the Jews (see Matt. 27: 37 // Mark 15:36 // Luke 23:37-38), are those who are crucified along with him, "one on his right and one on his left" (ἕνα ἐκ δεξιῶν καὶ ἕνα ἐξ εὐωνύμων αὐτοῦ [*hena ek dexiōn kai hena ex euōnymōn autou*]).[23] So in this, Jesus defines "true greatness" as he did at Matt. 16:24-28 and Mark 8:34-91 (cf. Luke 9:23-27), namely, as willingness to take up Jesus' cross.

Jesus thus defines true "greatness" as suffering service to others, not the exercise of dominion over others. For, according to Jesus, those who consider themselves to be the rulers of the nations do when they "lord it over" (κατακυριεύουσιν [*katakyrieuousin*]) their subjects and "exercise authority" (κατεξουσιάζουσιν) over them do not establish justice and peace, but treat those over whom they rule as if they were foes, and exploit them for their own personal advantage. Many in Jesus' day shared the vaunted Roman that claimed to bring the world "peace and security" through their "lording it over" the nations they conquered.[24]

---

22. "Taking account of what immediately follows, the sense [of Jesus' remark] appears to be as follows: you do not know that in requesting to participate in my glory you ask at the same time to share in my painful destiny" (William L. Lane, *The Gospel according to Mark*, New International Commentary on the Greek New Testament [Grand Rapids: Eerdmans, 1974], 379). See also David Hill, "The Request of Zebedee's Sons and the Johannine ΔΟΞΑ Theme," *New Testament Studies* 13 (1967): 281–85, esp. 284–85.
23. See Werner Kelber, *Mark's Story of Jesus* (Philadelphia: Fortress Press, 1979), 51.
24. Κατακυριεύω means "to become master over" or "to gain dominion over," and in its present context signifies the powerful and crippling rule of a mighty sovereign over a conquered people. The term κατεξουσιάζω literally means, as noted in the translation above, "to

Forgiveness

Jesus' teaching on forgiveness appears at Matt. 5:7; 6:14-15; 7:1-2 // Luke 6:37-38; Matt. 18:21-35; Mark 11:25; Luke 17:3-4; and, indirectly but powerfully, at Luke 23:33-34 (see table 4.5).

Matt. 5:7

Blessed are the merciful, for they will receive mercy.

Matt. 6:14-15

For if you forgive others their trespasses, your heavenly Father will also forgive you; but if you do not forgive others, neither will your Father forgive your trespasses.

Matt. 7:1-2 // Luke 6:37-38

Do not judge, so that you may not be judged. For with the judgment you make you will be judged, and the measure you give will be the measure you get.	Do not judge, and you will not be judged; do not condemn, and you will not be condemned. Forgive, and you will be forgiven; give, and it will be given to you. A good measure, pressed down, shaken together, running over, will be put into your lap; for the measure you give will be the measure you get back.

Matt. 18:21-35

Then Peter came and said to him, "Lord, if another member of the church sins against me, how often should I forgive? As many as seven times?" Jesus said to him, "Not seven times, but, I tell you, seventy-seven times. "For this reason the kingdom of heaven may be compared to a king who wished to settle accounts with his slaves. When he began the reckoning, one who owed him ten thousand talents was brought to him; and, as he could not pay, his lord ordered him to be sold, together with his wife and children and all his possessions, and payment to be made. So the slave fell on his knees before him, saying, 'Have patience with me, and I will pay you everything.' And out of pity for him, the lord of that slave released him and forgave him the debt. But that same slave, as he went out, came upon one of his fellow slaves who owed him a hundred denarii; and seizing him by the throat, he said, 'Pay what you owe.' Then his fellow slave fell down and pleaded with him, 'Have patience with me, and I will pay you.' But he refused; then he went and threw him into prison until he would pay the debt. When his fellow slaves saw what had happened, they were greatly distressed, and they went and reported to their lord all that had taken place. Then his lord summoned him and said to him, 'You wicked slave! I forgave you all that debt because you pleaded with me. Should you not have had mercy on your fellow slave, as I had mercy on you?'

---

tyrannize," "to exercise a power which tends toward compulsion and oppression." W. Foerster, "κατεξουσιάζω," *TDNT* 2:575.

And in anger his lord handed him over to be tortured until he would pay his entire debt. So my heavenly Father will also do to every one of you, if you do not forgive your brother or sister from your heart."

Luke 17:3-4

Be on your guard! If another disciple sins, you must rebuke the offender, and if there is repentance, you must forgive. And if the same person sins against you seven times a day, and turns back to you seven times and says, "I repent," you must forgive.

Mark 11:25

Whenever you stand praying, forgive, if you have anything against anyone; so that your Father in heaven may also forgive you your trespasses.

Luke 23:33-34

33 When they came to the place that is called The Skull, they crucified Jesus there with the criminals, one on his right and one on his left. [[34 Then Jesus said, "Father, forgive them; for they do not know what they are doing."]]

Table 4.5

These passages illustrate two things: first, to be included among the sons of God, a disciple must be willing to forgive even their enemies. Second, would-be sons who refuse to forgive their enemies exclude themselves from being or becoming "sons of God." Moreover, forgiveness is concretely related to repentance (Luke 24:47) and to a disciple's acceptance that the ways that Jesus proclaims as the way for Israel are indeed God's ways (Mark 2:5).

Peacemakers

Jesus' teaching on sons of God as εἰρηνοποιοί, "peacemakers," appears at two places in the Synoptic Gospels. At Matt. 5:9, in the Beatitudes, it stands as a preface to a series of antitheses on anger, judging, and retaliation, which are all examples of peacemaking (5:21-26).[25] At Matt. 5:38-48 // Luke 6:27-32, we find Jesus' teaching on love of enemies, which is, as a number of commentators have

---

25. So, *Sermon on the Mount*, 138.

noted,[26] paraenetically of a piece with Matt. 5:9 in having the same promise of "sonship" and the same combination of conduct with "sonship"—something found nowhere else in the New Testament (see table 4.6).

Matt. 5:9

Blessed are the peacemakers, for they will be called sons of God.

Matt. 5:21-24

You have heard that it was said to those of ancient times, "You shall not murder"; and "whoever murders shall be liable to judgment." But I say to you that if you are angry with a brother or sister, you will be liable to judgment; and if you insult a brother or sister, you will be liable to the council; and if you say, "You fool," you will be liable to the hell of fire. So when you are offering your gift at the altar, if you remember that your brother or sister has something against you, leave your gift there before the altar and go; first be reconciled to your brother or sister, and then come and offer your gift.

Matt. 5:38-42 // Luke 6:29-31

You have heard that it was said, "An eye for an eye and a tooth for a tooth." But I say to you, Do not resist an evildoer. But if anyone strikes you on the right cheek, turn the other also; and if anyone wants to sue you and take your coat, give your cloak as well; and if anyone forces you to go one mile, go also the second mile. Give to everyone who begs from you, and do not refuse anyone who wants to borrow from you.	If anyone strikes you on the cheek, offer the other also; and from anyone who takes away your coat do not withhold even your shirt. Give to everyone who begs from you; and if anyone takes away your goods, do not ask for them again. Do to others as you would have them do to you.

Matt. 5:43-48 // Luke 6:27-28, 32-36

You have heard that it was said, "You shall love your neighbor and hate your enemy." But I say to you, Love your enemies	But to you who are willing to listen, I say, love your enemies! Do good to those who hate you. Bless those who curse you.

---

26. Dieter Lührmann, "Liebet eure Feinde (Lk 6, 27–36/Mt 5, 39–48)," *Zeitschrift für Theologie und Kirche* 69 (1972): 412–38; Jacques Dupont, *Les Béatitudes*, vol. 3, *Les évangelistes* (Paris: Gabalda, 1973), 665–66. Robert Guelich, *The Sermon on the Mount: A Foundation for Understanding* (Waco, TX: Word, 1982), 91–92.

and pray for those who persecute you, so that you may be children of your Father in heaven; for he makes his sun rise on the evil and on the good, and sends rain on the righteous and on the unrighteous.	Pray for those who hurt you. . . .
For if you love those who love you, what reward do you have? Do not even the tax collectors do the same? And if you greet only your brothers and sisters, what more are you doing than others? Do not even the Gentiles do the same?	If you love only those who love you, why should you get credit for that? Even sinners love those who love them! And if you do good only to those who do good to you, why should you get credit? Even sinners do that much!
	And if you lend money only to those who can repay you, why should you get credit? Even sinners will lend to other sinners for a full return. Love your enemies! Do good to them. Lend to them without expecting to be repaid. Then your reward from heaven will be very great, and you will truly be acting as children of the Most High, for he is kind to those who are unthankful and wicked.
Be perfect, therefore, as your heavenly Father is perfect.	You must be compassionate, just as your Father is compassionate.

Table 4.6

It is interesting to note that, as H. Windisch has pointed out, Jesus' view of who and what a peacemaker is stands in stark contrast with the view, current in the Hellenistic world, of what this office entailed. Those who were to establish peace, security, and economic welfare were expected to do so only for their own people and through the conquest of their enemies.[27] As the texts above make clear, in Jesus' teaching, peacemakers are specifically those who do several things:

---

27. Windisch, "Friedensbringer—Gottessöhne," 240–60. The contrast seems intentional. Cf. Matt. 20:25-28 // Luke 24-27.

1. They make known to Israel and to the world the true nature and character of God, the type of devotion he demands, and his ways of dealing with human beings by acting as God acts, especially in his dealings with the ἄδικοι (*adikoi*), "the unjust" or "wicked," as opposed to the "righteous."
2. They have committed themselves to living a life in accordance with a higher, divinely demanded δικαιοσύνη (*dikaiosynē*), a "righteousness" that is specifically exhibited in refraining from killing and anger, from lust and covetousness, from retaliation of injury, and especially from hatred of the enemy.
3. They bring God's peace into the world by being compassionate as God is compassionate, not just to his own but also to those who should not have any (or have forfeited their) right to that compassion.
4. They mirror and manifest the very character of God specifically and most definitively by "loving the enemy."[28]

Jesus is presented not only as calling those who aspire to be true sons of God to imitate God specifically in his displays of indiscriminate mercy to the "wicked" but also as declaring that conduct to be worthy of the office and title of a "true child of God." To be called and appointed by God to this office and title, one must acknowledge that the path of nonviolence, nonretaliation, and, preeminently, active love and concern for the enemy is the path "of God."[29]

---

28. On these as the characteristics of the peacemakers spoken of by Jesus in Matt. 5:9, see B. W. Bacon, "The Blessing of the Peacemakers," *Expository Times* 41 (1929/1930): 58–60; Windisch, "Friedensbringer—Gottessöhn," 240–41; Foerster, "εἰρηνοποιός," *TDNT* 2:419; Robert A. Guelich, *The Sermon on the Mount: A Foundation for Understanding* (Waco: Word, 1982), 92.
29. On this, see John Piper, *Love Your Enemies: Jesus' Love Command in the Synoptic Gospels and the Early Christian Paraenesis* (Cambridge: Cambridge University Press, 1980), 62; and the discussion of the links between sonship, *imitatio dei*, indiscriminate mercy, nonviolence/nonretaliation, and love of enemies in the teaching of the Jesus in Marcus J. Borg, *Conflict, Holiness and Politics in the Teaching of Jesus* (Harrisburg, PA: Trinity Press International, 1998), 136–46.

To be a son of God, then, is to act in the world as God does, showing mercy and forgiveness toward all, refusing to retaliate injury for injury, accepting suffering and persecution as the price of living in conformity to God's will, and, most importantly, loving and not "hating" (seeking or willing the destruction of) those ordinarily deemed the enemies of Israel.

With all of this in mind, let's return to our questions: Why did Jesus call disciples in the first place, and why did he think it was necessary to have them?

Why Disciples?

Thankfully, the question of why Jesus called and gathered disciples is easily answerable. We have multiple lines of evidence in the Gospels that allow us to speak confidently on the matter. The answer is that Jesus needed disciples in order to accomplish the purposes for which he felt himself divinely "tasked."[30] What were those purposes?

If we accept what the Gospels say in this regard, Jesus' purposes had nothing to do, as we may have become accustomed to thinking, with offering individuals a new way of salvation, especially one that involves "accepting Jesus into one's heart as one's personal Savior" or believing certain doctrinal assertions about him (that he is the second person of the blessed Trinity, for instance). Nor did they entail the fulfillment of some plan or necessity for him to die in order to save individuals from their sins by acting as a substitute for us before the bar of God's justice and enduring in anyone's stead the wrath and mortal punishment for sin. That specific understanding of Jesus' atoning death has long been prevalent in Western theological thought; it owes to Augustine the notion that every individual since Adam actually deserves to suffer for Adam's sin, but the specific

---

30. Caird, *New Testament Theology*, 361.

theological explanation of the aim of Jesus' "coming" for the purpose of a substitutionary death does not find expression anywhere, let alone in the Gospels, until the twelfth century of our era, in a writing of St. Anselm titled *Cur Deus Homo* (*Why God Become Man*). Anselm was intent to answer a theological, not historical, question raised by the doctrine of the incarnation, a question that presupposes a view of the person of Jesus from the perspective of a developed trinitarian theology. That theology is wholly anachronistic to any New Testament writing.

Rather, the Gospel authors present Jesus' purpose in calling disciples as something centered on making the people of Israel aware of three things:

1. That they were at a point in their national history in which their world was in grave danger of coming to an end.
2. That they must choose between two conceptions of how they should live as God's people: one that Jesus saw as rooted in a way of being Israel that he called "setting [one's] mind on human things" (Mark 8:33), a way that in Jesus' view was guided by a policy of nationalism that would lead, as historically it did, to the destruction of the Jewish nation. The other, the one he advocated, entailed the principle of being merciful as God was merciful, a way that Israel would need to accept if they were to escape what John the Baptizer had called "the wrath to come."
3. That they had little time left to them to make that choice.

Accordingly, Jesus called disciples because he knew that this task was beyond the ability of one man to accomplish. If he were to have any chance at all of actually making Israel aware of the national emergency that confronted it, he had to have others besides himself who would act as he was acting and would be, to quote my teacher

George Caird, "couriers proclaiming a national emergency and conducting a national referendum on a question of national survival."[31]

But Jesus called and gathered disciples for another reason as well: to found what sociologists have called "intentional communities," small groups and cells of followers, some living within their home villages and towns, some on the road as itinerants. These cells would, by living out a particular kind of corporate life consistent with the path of faithfulness to God that he was calling Israel to adopt, make incarnate his vision of what faithful Israel should look like.[32] This must not, mind you, be in any way understood as something tantamount to a desire on Jesus' part to found a church. For as far as Jesus was concerned, there already was a "church," one he wholeheartedly belonged to, namely, the ἐκκλησία κυρίου (*ekklēsia kyriou*), the "congregation of the Lord," that is, the people of Israel.[33] Moreover, he never spoke of the group he called into being except in terms of titles used previously by the prophets and his contemporaries to designate the people of Israel, one of which was, notably, "son" or "sons of God." Rather, he called and gathered disciples around himself in order to accomplish what he believed was another task given to him by God, namely, to reconstitute Israel and to rescue it from what he and other figures of his day called the "wrath to come," that is, the judgment, often embodied in national calamity, that the prophets declared was inevitable for Israel if they were persistent in covenant unfaithfulness. Without creating and having with him an actual core of followers who would answer his summons to Israel to be the true people (as distinct from "persons") of God by taking it up and heeding it corporately, he would fail to accomplish his mission.

---

31. Caird, *New Testament Theology*, 361.
32. Wright, *Jesus and the Victory of God*, 276, 317.
33. On this, see K. L. Schmidt, "ἐκκλησία," *TDNT* 3:526.

For proof of this last point, we only need note that each of the Synoptic evangelists, particularly in their respective stories of the Last Supper and of Jesus in Gethsemane, takes pains to depict Jesus as feeling that his mission had come to naught because he had failed to attract any large following, and because he knew that one of his few remaining followers (Judas) had betrayed him and that all of the others, including his closest followers (Peter, James, and John), were on the verge of deserting him and his cause when he most needed them.

Masters, Disciples, and Prayers

But why, then, instruct the disciples *in prayer*? It obviously cannot be because Jesus desired to teach his disciples that, contrary to what they might otherwise think, they had an obligation to pray, or that there was such a thing as prayer. As Jews, they would have already known these things, for Jews were, and for centuries had been, a people of prayer. Rather, it was for two other purposes. First of all, Jesus sought to characterize and shape them as *his* disciples. Second, he intended to keep them from falling away from or rejecting everything with which they, as his disciples, were to align themselves; only in this way would they stand in contrast to the ways of those in Israel whom Jesus called "this generation." Let's see how this is so.

That Jesus' purpose in giving his disciples the Disciples' Prayer was to characterize and shape them as *his* disciples is something we know because the first and third evangelists tell us so, albeit in different ways. Matthew does this by placing Jesus' giving of the Disciples' Prayer to his disciples within a long discourse by Jesus (Matthew 5–7) in which Jesus is presented as a new Moses who, like the old, gives the people of God the particular way they should arrange themselves corporately as God's people. More specifically, Matthew locates the prayer in a section of this discourse devoted to how those should pray who wish not to be like "the hypocrites," but to faithfully follow Jesus (Matt. 6:5-8). As we've already noted, Luke makes the occasion of Jesus' giving the Disciples' Prayer a request from an unnamed disciple who, after having seen Jesus himself at prayer, asks Jesus to give those who are following him, both literally and figuratively, a prayer that in function "is like the one that John [the Baptizer] gave to his disciples" (Luke 11:1, my translation), that is to say, one that will characterize their position as a community around Jesus and that will express the distinctive piety into which Jesus has drawn the disciple band. Indeed, that this would be Jesus' purpose in giving his disciples a prayer of their own is hardly surprising, since other Jewish teachers in Jesus' time also shaped their disciples by giving them a distinctive prayer.[34]

The Center of Jesus' and the Disciples' Petitionary Prayers

Jesus also gave his disciples the Disciples' Prayer in order to keep them from falling away from and abandoning all with which they, as his disciples, were to align themselves. They might have done this by going over to the ways of being Israel that Jesus was calling the Jewish nation to reject. To support this point, I observe, first, that a concern to secure divine aid against apostasy lies at the center of all other explicitly petitionary prayers that Jesus himself is said to have prayed. Second, the Disciples' Prayer was not the only prayer Jesus urged his disciples to pray. There were four other prayers, each also petitionary or commanding in nature, and each of them, notably, was to be uttered in times of urgency or crisis. We find at the center of these other prayers a concern to secure for the disciples divine aid to ensure that they do not engage in apostasy. I turn next to these prayers.

---

34. So Alfred Plummer, *A Critical and Exegetical Commentary on the Gospel according to St. Luke* (London: T&T Clark, 1909), 293; Betz, *Sermon on the Mount*, 377.

The Center of Jesus' Prayers

Matthew portrays Jesus as engaged in petitionary prayer only once, at Matt. 26:39-44.[35] Luke does so three times, at Luke 22:32;[36] 22:41-42, 45;[37] and 23:34.[38] There can be little doubt that the Matthean and first two Lukan instances of Jesus engaged in petitionary prayer have Jesus praying for aid from God to avoid apostasy. Jesus' prayer in Gethsemane or the Mount of Olives (Matt. 26:39-44 and Luke 22:41-42, 45) is a plea to be rid of the exigencies of his divine vocation, yet nevertheless to have his will conformed to that of God. Jesus' prayer (in Luke 22:32) for Simon Peter, whom Satan, Jesus says, has demanded to "have" and to "sift" like wheat, is that the apostle will be guarded by God from failing in faithfulness.[39]

But what of the third Lukan instance, Luke 23:24, in which Jesus is presented as asking God to forgive those who have inflicted the outrage of the cross on his Son? At first glance, it seems unlikely that the center of this prayer has anything to do with the securing of divine aid against falling into apostasy. Those for whom Jesus prays have already shown themselves to be disobedient to the divine will. And yet, since the outrage is labeled as something done through

---

35. "And going a little farther he fell on his face and prayed, 'My Father, if it be possible, let this cup pass from me; nevertheless, not as I will, but as thou wilt.' And he came to the disciples and found them sleeping; and he said to Peter, 'So, could you not watch with me one hour? Watch and pray that you may not enter into temptation; the spirit indeed is willing, but the flesh is weak.' Again, for the second time, he went away and prayed, 'My Father, if this cannot pass unless I drink it, thy will be done.' And again he came and found them sleeping, for their eyes were heavy. So, leaving them again, he went away and prayed for the third time, saying the same words" (RSV).
36. "Simon, Simon, behold, Satan demanded to have you, that he might sift you like wheat, but I have prayed for you that your faith may not fail; and when you have turned again, strengthen your brethren" (RSV).
37. "And he withdrew from them about a stone's throw, and knelt down and prayed, 'Father, if thou art willing, remove this cup from me; nevertheless not my will, but thine, be done'" (RSV).
38. "And Jesus said, 'Father, forgive them; for they know not what they do.' And they cast lots to divide his garments" (RSV).
39. On this, see Oscar Cullmann, *Prayer in the New Testament* (Minneapolis: Fortress Press, 1995), 27.

inadvertence, there is here at least the implicit notion that those responsible for Jesus' crucifixion could yet come to realize the enormity of their offense, and consequently repent of the deed, if they could be jarred to their senses about what it is they do. Now, according to Luke, what jars a sinner to the realization that he or she has abandoned the ways of God, and therefore what gives him or her the opportunity to turn to God in true obedience, is the experience of God's forgiveness, as his story of the repentant woman (which includes the parable of the two debtors in Luke 7:36-50) shows. So Luke 23:34, too, actually is concerned with the securing of divine aid against apostasy; for in praying for God to forgive those responsible for the crucifixion, Jesus is calling out to God to give them what is necessary to renounce their disobedience and become truly conformed to the divine will.[40]

The Other "Disciples' Prayers" and Their Focus

The other prayers Jesus gave his disciples to recite are recorded (1) at Matt. 9:38 // Luke 10:2, at the beginning of the story of Jesus commissioning his disciples to go out to Israel and engage in the mission that he himself was commissioned to undertake (Matt. 9:35-10:42 // Luke 10:1-16); (2) at Matt. 24:20, in a section of Matthew's Gospel usually labeled "the eschatological discourse"; (3) at Luke 21:36, in a similarly titled section of his Gospel; and (4) at

---

40. I cannot help but wonder whether Luke did not also mean for us to see Jesus here as petitioning God for protection against *his own* (i.e., Jesus') apostasy. In the first place, when Jesus utters the petition "Father, forgive them for they know not what they do" he not only calls on God to show mercy to those who are responsible for his crucifixion but also engages in the very thing that at Luke 11:3 (!) he has told his disciples they must do in order to ensure receiving that which God gives to prevent his elect from becoming estranged from him. Does this not imply, then, (1) that prior to, and as the occasion of, uttering his prayer Jesus feels himself to be on the verge of apostasy and (2) that the prayer is made to secure divine aid against apostasy for himself as well as for others?

Mark 14:38 // Matt. 26:41 // Luke 22:40, 46, in the story of Jesus in Gethsemane.[41] See table 4.7 for these texts in context.

Matt. 9:35—10:7 // Luke 10:1–11

And Jesus went about all the cities and villages, teaching in their synagogues and preaching the gospel of the kingdom, and healing every disease and every infirmity. When he saw the crowds, he had compassion for them, because they were harassed and helpless, like sheep without a shepherd.	After this the Lord appointed seventy others, and sent them on ahead of him, two by two, into every town and place where he himself was about to come.
Then he said to his disciples, "The harvest is plentiful, but the laborers are few; pray therefore the Lord of the harvest to send out laborers into his harvest."	*And he said to them, "The harvest is plentiful, but the laborers are few; pray therefore the Lord of the harvest to send out laborers into his harvest.*
And he called to him his twelve disciples and gave them authority over unclean spirits, to cast them out, and to heal every disease and every infirmity. . . . These twelve Jesus sent out, charging them, "Go nowhere among the Gentiles, and enter no town of the Samaritans, but go rather to the lost sheep of the house of Israel.	Go your way; behold, I send you out as lambs in the midst of wolves. Carry no purse, no bag, no sandals; and salute no one on the road. Whatever house you enter, first say, 'Peace be to this house!' And if a son of peace is there, your peace shall rest upon him; but if not, it shall return to you. And remain in the same house, eating and drinking what they provide, for the laborer deserves his wages; do not go from house to house. Whenever you enter a town and they receive you, eat what is set before you;
And preach as you go, saying, 'The kingdom of heaven is at hand.'"	heal the sick in it and say to them, 'The kingdom of God has come near to you.' But whenever you enter a town and they do not receive you, go into its streets and say, 'Even the dust of your town that clings to our feet, we wipe off against you; nevertheless know this, that the kingdom of God has come near.'"

---

41. One might wish to argue that Matt. 5:44, "But I say to you, Love your enemies and pray for those who persecute you . . . ", should be included among these instances. But I think it is to be excluded on the grounds that no instruction regarding what it is the disciples are to ask God for with respect to their persecutors is stated.

THE DISCIPLES' PRAYER

Matt. 24:15-21

So when you see the desolating sacrilege spoken of by the prophet Daniel, standing in the holy place (let the reader understand), then let those who are in Judea flee to the mountains; let him who is on the housetop not go down to take what is in his house; and let him who is in the field not turn back to take his mantle. And alas for those who are with child and for those who give suck in those days! *Pray that your flight may not be in winter or on a sabbath.* For then there will be great tribulation, such as has not been from the beginning of the world until now, no, and never will be.

Luke 21:20-36

"But when you see Jerusalem surrounded by armies, then know that its desolation has come near. Then let those who are in Judea flee to the mountains, and let those who are inside the city depart, and let not those who are out in the country enter it; for these are days of vengeance, to fulfill all that is written. Alas for those who are with child and for those who give suck in those days! For great distress shall be upon the earth and wrath upon this people; they will fall by the edge of the sword, and be led captive among all nations; and Jerusalem will be trodden down by the Gentiles, until the times of the Gentiles are fulfilled.

"And there will be signs in sun and moon and stars, and upon the earth distress of nations in perplexity at the roaring of the sea and the waves, men fainting with fear and with foreboding of what is coming on the world; for the powers of the heavens will be shaken. And then they will see the Son of man coming in a cloud with power and great glory. Now when these things begin to take place, look up and raise your heads, because your redemption is drawing near."

And he told them a parable: "Look at the fig tree, and all the trees; as soon as they come out in leaf, you see for yourselves and know that the summer is already near. So also, when you see these things taking place, you know that the kingdom of God is near. Truly, I say to you, this generation will not pass away till all has taken place. Heaven and earth will pass away, but my words will not pass away.

"But take heed to yourselves lest your hearts be weighed down with dissipation and drunkenness and cares of this life, and that day come upon you suddenly like a snare; for it will come upon all who dwell upon the face of the whole earth. But watch at all times, praying that you may have strength to escape all these things that will take place, and to stand before the Son of man." But watch at all times, praying that you may have strength to escape all these things that will take place, and to stand before the Son of man."

Mark 14:32-42 // Matt. 26:36-46 // Luke 22:40-46

They went to a place called Gethsemane; and he said to his disciples,	Then Jesus went with them to a place called Gethsemane; and he said to his disciples,	"Pray that you may not come into the time of trial."

"Sit here while I pray." He took with him Peter and James and John, and began to be distressed and agitated. And he said to them, "I am deeply grieved, even to death; remain here, and keep awake."	"Sit here while I go over there and pray." He took with him Peter and the two sons of Zebedee, and began to be grieved and agitated. Then he said to them, "I am deeply grieved, even to death; remain here, and stay awake with me."	
And going a little farther, he threw himself on the ground and prayed that, if it were possible, the hour might pass from him.	And going a little farther, he threw himself on the ground and prayed,	Then he withdrew from them about a stone's throw, knelt down, and prayed,
He said, "Abba, Father, for you all things are possible; remove this cup from me; yet, not what I want, but what you want."	"My Father, if it is possible, let this cup pass from me; yet not what I want but what you want."	"Father, if you are willing, remove this cup from me; yet, not my will but yours be done." . . .
He came and found them sleeping; and he said to Peter, "Simon, are you asleep? Could you not keep awake one hour? Keep awake and pray that you may not come into πειρασμόν; the spirit indeed is willing, but the flesh is weak."	Then he came to the disciples and found them sleeping; and he said to Peter, "So, could you not stay awake with me one hour? Stay awake and pray that you may not come into πειρασμόν; the spirit indeed is willing, but the flesh is weak."	When he got up from prayer, he came to the disciples and found them sleeping because of grief, and he said to them, "Why are you sleeping? Get up and pray that you may not come into πειρασμόν."
And again he went away and prayed, saying the same words.	Again he went away for the second time and prayed, "My Father, if this cannot pass unless I drink it, your will be done."	
And once more he came and found them sleeping, for their eyes were very heavy; and they did not know what to say to him.	Again he came and found them sleeping, for their eyes were heavy. So leaving them again, he went away and prayed for the third time, saying the same words.	

He came a third time and said to them, "Are you still sleeping and taking your rest? Enough! The hour has come; the Son of Man is betrayed into the hands of sinners. Get up, let us be going. See, my betrayer is at hand."	Then he came to the disciples and said to them, "Are you still sleeping and taking your rest? See, the hour is at hand, and the Son of Man is betrayed into the hands of sinners. Get up, let us be going. See, my betrayer is at hand."

Table 4.7

What Jesus urges his disciples to pray for at Mark 14:38 // Matt. 26:41 // Luke 22:40, 46, as he begs God to prevent them from "entering into πειρασμός," "testing" or "trial," is divine aid against apostasy. To "enter into πειρασμός" is, as we will see more fully below,[42] at the very least to fall away from obedience to God, if not also to do what true sons of God are forbidden to do, namely, to put God to the test.

Jesus also urges his disciples to petition God for divine aid against apostasy at Matt. 24:20, where he instructs the disciples to beg God to ensure that the flight they must undertake when Jerusalem falls not be in winter or on a Sabbath. The "winter" (i.e., the rainy season of flooded wadis and muddy roads) and "Sabbath" (the day when rabbinic restrictions, suspension of services to travelers, and the inability to purchase supplies hindered flight) were situations that would place those who would be obedient to God's commands in peril of their lives, and would thus make disobedience attractive.[43] At Luke 21:36, the commanded object of prayer is for "strength to escape all these things" that will take place during the judgment that Jesus predicts will befall Jerusalem. "These things" are the trials of faithfulness mentioned in Luke 21:10-18 that the disciples have been destined to face.[44]

---

42. See pp. 153-55, where I argue on linguistic and other grounds that "to enter into πειρασμός" is not to experience subjection to a "test" or a "trial" but to engage in "testing" someone.
43. Robert H. Gundry, *Matthew: A Commentary on His Literary and Theological Art* (Grand Rapids: Eerdmans, 1982), 483.

Then he said to them, "Nation will rise against nation, and kingdom against kingdom; there will be great earthquakes, and in various places famines and pestilences; and there will be terrors and great signs from heaven. But before all this they will lay their hands on you and persecute you, delivering you up to the synagogues and prisons, and you will be brought before kings and governors for my name's sake. This will be a time for you to bear testimony. Settle it therefore in your minds, not to meditate beforehand how to answer; for I will give you a mouth and wisdom, which none of your adversaries will be able to withstand or contradict. You will be delivered up even by parents and brothers and kinsmen and friends, and some of you they will put to death; you will be hated by all for my name's sake.

But what about Matt. 9:38 and its Lukan counterpart in Luke 10:2? Here Jesus encourages the disciples to "beg" (δεήθητε [*deēthēte*], from δέομαι [*deomai*] = "to ask for with urgency," with the implication of presumed need; "to plead") God to swell their ranks so the golden opportunity, which according to Jesus is now and only briefly upon them, to complete the task of gathering Israel into God's kingdom is not forever lost. Is the focus of this prayer also the securing of divine aid to forestall apostasy? The answer becomes clear when we look at the prayer from the reverse angle, that is to say, from the point of view of its *non*fulfillment, and take into account what would surely happen to the disciples if God did not accede to their request for additional "laborers into his harvest." The disciples would be overwhelmed by the immensity of their assigned task and despair of ever completing it. Thus, in the light of this observation, the disciples' begging God to give them additional laborers is tantamount to asking for aid to avoid falling away. So here, too, as in the rest of the instances of prayers urged on the disciples by Jesus, the focus of these prayers is securing divine aid against apostasy.

---

44. On this, see John Nolland, *Luke 18:35—24:53*, Word Biblical Commentary (Dallas: Word, 1993), 1013.

Surely these observations show us that Jesus gave his disciples the Disciples' Prayer in order to keep them from falling away from, and abandoning, all that they were to commit themselves to if they were to be Jesus' disciples and aid him in his mission. If all of the other prayers that Jesus urged on his disciples have securing divine aid against apostasy as their focus, it would be very odd if this were not also the focus of the Disciples' Prayer.

One other consideration leads me to regard the protection of the disciples from apostasy as Jesus' purpose in giving them the Disciples' Prayer: the particular contexts into which Matthew and Luke have set Jesus' giving of the Disciples' Prayer to his disciples portray Jesus as vitally concerned precisely with teaching his disciples how to avoid apostasy.

The Contexts of the Prayer

As we have already seen, the larger context of Matt. 6:9-11, the Disciples' Prayer, is Matt. 5:1—7:28, the so-called Sermon on the Mount. Notably, this is a text in which the disciples (here specifically portrayed as fledgling "sons of God" and as salt and light) are given a new ethic that is, in content, often specifically formulated in terms of not being like the "hypocrites" or "the men of old" or "this generation" (that is, those of Jesus' coreligionists who, according to Jesus, have become apostate). The disciples are also (1) addressed as ones in imminent danger of being turned from this ethic by persecution (Matt. 5:11-12, 13-15; 6:25-33; 7:15-16a) and (2) sternly warned not to slacken in either the ways of being faithful to God that Jesus is teaching them or their confidence that God is faithful (Matt. 5:13-14, 21-47; 6:19-34; 7:7-11).

The context of Luke's version of the Disciples' Prayer is the first portion of Luke's presentation of the "exodus" of Jesus from Galilee to Jerusalem (Luke 9:51—18:14). Here Jesus not only emphasizes how his disciples and other would-be followers are to hear and do the will of God as he has spelled it out for them,[45] but also, as Darrell Bock has pointed out, holds up the behavior and unfaithfulness of "this generation" as the paradigm of how *not* to do this.[46]

In setting the Disciples' Prayer in these respective contexts, then, and thereby indicating that this prayer is thematically and functionally of a piece with the teaching Jesus gives there on how to avoid becoming apostate, Matthew and Luke suggest that Jesus' purpose in giving the Disciples' Prayer to his disciples had something to do with girding and guarding them against engaging in apostasy.

My argument, however, is not just that Jesus gave the Disciples' Prayer as a means of protecting his disciples from apostasy. It is also that the apostasy from which he sought to safeguard them entailed their potential going over to the ways of being Israel that Jesus was calling the Jewish nation to reject. Here two observations are relevant. The first is that, throughout the Gospels, Jesus uses language taken from Psalm 95 and other biblical accounts of Israel's wilderness rebellions in order to speak of the ways for being Israel that he rejects, the ways he attributes to "this generation."[47] The second is something I've already noted, namely, that Jesus often frames his warnings to his disciples in terms of the dangerous influence of the "teachings" that "this generation" propagates in word and deed. If the disciples are to achieve their corporate identity as his disciples, it is absolutely necessary that they not let themselves come under that influence. Surely this shows that, in Jesus' eyes, to turn away from what he

---

45. See Bo Reike, "Instruction and Discussion in the Travel Narrative," *Studia Evangelica* 1 (Texte und Untersuchungen 73) (1959): 206–16.
46. "In the first portion of the section, there is an interchange between debate with the Jewish leadership and instruction on discipleship. Jesus points to the Jewish leadership as an example of how *not* to walk with God" (Darrell Bock, *The Gospel of Luke* [Grand Rapids: Baker Book House, 1996]), 2:964.
47. On these texts as the source of Jesus' "this generation" language, see E. Lövestam, *Jesus and "This Generation": A New Testament Study* (Stockholm: Almqvist & Wiksell, 1995).

taught and to deny or abandon him and his ways is to become a member of "this generation."

But what clinches the case is the implication of a fact I will explore more fully in the next chapter: that each of the individual petitions of the Disciples' Prayer not only recalls but also appears to be set out in (conscious?) contradistinction to the description of the wilderness prototype of "this generation." The "wilderness generation" was called by a messenger of God (Moses) to be God's people by following the ways this messenger had proclaimed. Yet it refused to sanctify God's name and instead profaned it (Num 20:12; 27:14). It did not do God's will (Psalm 95). It called on God to stop giving them the "bread for the morrow" it received from him, and with which it should have been satisfied (Num. 11:1-6; Ps. 78:17-18). And it put God to the test (Exod. 17:1-9; Deut. 6:16; Ps. 78:40-41; 95:1-11; 106:14).

Why would Jesus make reference to all of this, and why would he frame the petitions of the prayer he gave his disciples in terms of not doing what the biblical prototype of "this generation" does, unless he was trying to give to his disciples something that would help them avoid becoming like them?

The Prayer's Occasion

There remains one more question to be answered. Why would Jesus trouble himself to aid his disciples in this way? Was there some fear or anticipation on his part that the disciples were attracted to the ways of "this generation"—or, even worse, were actually likely to go over to its side? If we can trust the Gospel authors on this matter, the answer is an unequivocal yes. For they report that Jesus himself said as much. This is quite clear in the evangelists' stories of the Last Supper, where Jesus lets his disciples know that he is aware, first, that one of his own, Judas, is about to fulfill a previously formulated plan to betray him to members of "this generation" (Matt. 26:20-29; Mark 14:17-25; Luke 22:14-38) (see table 4.8). (Note that from the time he is first named, when he is called by Jesus to be among the Twelve, Judas is never spoken of in the Gospels without some reference to his eventual act of "handing Jesus over" to Jesus' enemies.)

Matt. 26:20-25; Mark 14:17-21; Luke 22:14, 21-23

Matt. 26:20-25	Mark 14:17-21	Luke 22:14, 21-23
When it was evening, he took his place with the twelve;	When it was evening, he came with the twelve. And when they had taken their places	When the hour came, he took his place at the table, and the apostles with him....
and while they were eating, he said, "Truly I tell you, one of you will betray me."	and were eating, Jesus said, "Truly I tell you, one of you will betray me, one who is eating with me."	But see, the one who betrays me is with me, and his hand is on the table....
And they became greatly distressed and began to say to him one after another, "Surely not I, Lord?" He answered, "The one who has dipped his hand into the bowl with me will betray me.	They began to be distressed and to say to him one after another, "Surely, not I?" He said to them, "It is one of the twelve, one who is dipping bread into the bowl with me.	
The Son of Man goes as it is written of him, but woe to that one by whom the Son of Man is betrayed! It would have been better for that one not to have been born."	For the Son of Man goes as it is written of him, but woe to that one by whom the Son of Man is betrayed! It would have been better for that one not to have been born."	For the Son of Man is going as it has been determined, but woe to that one by whom he is betrayed!"
Judas, who betrayed him, said, "Surely not I, Rabbi?" He replied, "You have said so."	Then they began to ask one another, which one of them it could be who would do this.	

Table 4.8

Second, as is noted in Luke 21:31-32, Jesus not only felt compelled to pray for Peter and the disciples that their faithfulness to God may not fail, but also knew that their faithfulness was in need of strengthening: "Simon, Simon, listen! Satan has demanded to sift all of you like wheat, but I have prayed for you that your own faith may not fail; and you, when once you have turned back, strengthen your brothers." It is also manifest in the stories of Jesus with his disciples at Gethsemane (Matt. 26:30–35 // Mark 14:26–31 // Luke 22:39), wherein Jesus notes that there is now grave danger that "You will all become deserters because of me this night; for it is written, 'I will strike the shepherd, and the sheep of the flock will be scattered'" (Matt. 26:31; cf. Mark 14:27). When push came to shove, Peter would not be able to live up to his own words that he was ready to follow Jesus to prison and to death and that, no matter what any other of the disciples did, he would always remain staunchly loyal (see Matt. 26:33 // Mark 14:29 // Luke 22:33). He would instead deny him—and more than once (Matt. 26:34 // Mark 14:30 // Luke 22:34). Jesus also evidently feels the need to urge the disciples to "Stay awake and pray that you may not come into 'temptation' (Matt. 26:41a // Mark 14:38a // Luke 22:40:46), and to warn them that with respect to falling into apostasy, they are weak (Matt. 24:41b // Mark 14:38b).

But more importantly for our purposes, Jesus displays this knowledge and fear that the disciples were both attracted to the ways of "this generation" and were at risk of, if not actually engaged in, going over to its side throughout his ministry—indeed, from immediately after he called them to follow him up to his arrest, trial, and execution. Consider, for instance, how just shortly after he called and commissioned his disciples Jesus notes that the disciples did not understand his teaching in his parable of the sower about how his Gospel message must be spread to all and sundry, because they were aligning themselves with "those outside"—that is, those among Israel who have hardened their hearts to his message. Consider, too, how at Matt. 16:6, 8-12, and Mark 8:15 (cf. Luke 12:1), after his display of God's mercy to gentiles in the feeding of the five thousand,

Jesus warns the disciples against falling prey to the teaching of the members of "this generation." Then, at Matt. 16:8-11 // Mark 8:17-21, he castigates them for developing the same "hardness of heart" (πώρωσις [*pōrōsis*]) and culpable lack of "perception" (νόημα [*noēma*]) and "understanding" (σύνεσις [*synesis*]) that those who "are outside" possess (cf. Matt. 13:13-14 // Mark 4:11-12 // 8:10), and for displaying attitudes toward his mission that are characteristic of those who oppose it.[48] Also remember, when at Caesarea Philippi, which Mark and Luke present as a turning point in Jesus' ministry, how powerfully and in what connotative terms Jesus excoriates his disciples, through Peter, for showing themselves to be going over to the side of "men" (= Jesus opponents). They have not remained on God's side, after they balk at his declaration that God has set for his Messiah and all those who would follow him a destiny of suffering and death at the hands of their enemies rather than their triumphing over them.

> And Jesus went on with his disciples, to the villages of Caesarea Philippi; and on the way he asked his disciples, "Who do men say that I am?" And they told him, "John the Baptist; and others say, Elijah; and others one of the prophets." And he asked them, "But who do you say that I am?" Peter answered him, "You are the Christ." And he charged them to tell no one about him.

> And he began to teach them that the Son of man must suffer many things, and be rejected by the elders and the chief priests and the scribes, and be killed, and after three days rise again. And he said this plainly.

---

48. On this, see my "The Rebuke of the Disciples in Mark 8.14-21," *Journal for the Study of the New Testament* 8 (1986): 31–47; Kelly Iverson, *Gentiles in the Gospel of Mark: "Even the Dogs under the Table Eat the Children's Crumbs"* (London: T&T Clark, 2007), 95–97; J. Ted Blakely, "Incomprehension or Resistance? The Markan Disciples and the Narrative logic of Mark 4:1—8:30" (PhD diss., St. Andrews University, 2008), http://research-repository.st-andrews.ac.uk/handle/10023/566; Blakely's thesis takes "as its starting point an argument" that I made in the article cited above "that the harshness of Jesus' rebuke in Mark 8:14-21 is occasioned not by the disciples' lack of faith or incomprehension but by their active resistance to his Gentile mission."

> And Peter took him, and began to rebuke him. But turning and seeing his disciples, he rebuked Peter, and said, "Get behind me, Satan! For you are not on the side of God, but of men." (Mark 8:27-31)

Moreover, going over to the side of "this generation" is exactly what all the disciples ended up actually doing in one way or another when the consequences of following Jesus's ways were brought home to them on the night of Jesus' arrest and trial.

The Aim of the Prayer

So what was it that Jesus thought his disciples would be praying for if they followed his instructions and prayed the prayer he gave them?

The answer most frequently given by scholars is one that, so far as I can tell, was first given by Johannes Weiss in the wake of his (and others') "rediscovery" of "apocalyptic" at the end of the nineteenth century. Weiss made the claim that the view of an impending "end of the age" was central, rather than peripheral, to the Judaism of Jesus' time and to the teaching and ministry of Jesus himself.[49] Weiss's claim has "ruled the roost" in almost all discussions of the Disciples' Prayer ever since.[50] On this common view, Jesus intended his disciples to

---

49. See Johannes Weiss, *Die Predigt Jesu vom Reiche Gottes* (Göttingen; Vandenhoeck & Ruprecht, 1892).
50. See, for instance, those of Ernst Lohmeyer (*The Lord's Prayer* [London: Collins, 1965]), Joachim Jeremias (*The Lord's Prayer* [Philadelphia: Fortress Press, 1964], 17–33), Raymond E. Brown ("The Pater Noster as an Eschatological Prayer," in *New Testament Essays* [Garden City, NY: Doubleday, 1968], 275–320), John P. Meier (*A Marginal Jew: Rethinking the Historical Jesus*, vol. 2, *Mentor, Message, and Miracles* [New York: Doubleday, 1994], 291–302), among many others, e.g., T. H. Zahn, *Das Evangelium des Matthäus* (Leipzig: Diechert, 1903), 268–274; Albert Schweitzer (*The Mysticism of Paul the Apostle* [New York: Macmillan, 1955]), R. Eisler ("Das letzte Abendmahl," *Zeitschrift für die neutestamentliche Wissenschaft und die Kunde der älteren Kirche* 24 [1925]: 190–92); Rudolf Bultmann (*Jesus and the Word* [New York: Charles Scribner's Sons, 1934], 181); H. Greeven (*Gebet und Eschatologie im Neuen Testament*, Neutestamentliche Forschungen III/1 [Gütersloh: Bertelesmann, 1931], 72–101); H. Schürmann (*Praying with Christ: The "Our Father" for Today* [New York: Herder & Herder, 1964]); S. Schulz, *Q: Die Spruchquelle der Evangelisten* [Zurich: Theologischer Verlag, 1972], 84–93), and to a large extent A. Vögtle ("Der 'eschatologische' Bezug der Wir-Bitten des Vaterunser," in *Jesus und Paulus*, ed. E. Ellis and E. Grässer [Göttingen: Vandenhoeck & Ruprecht, 1975], 344–62), Norman

pray, in the prayer he gave them, for the blessings that many first-century Jews apparently believed properly belonged to "the world to come," blessings that would be ushered in by God and distributed to the faithful people of Israel after God brought history to its intended climax and established once and for all his kingdom of peace and justice on earth. I quote two prominent representatives of this view, W. D. Davies and Dale C. Allison:

> Matt. 6:9-13 par. is from beginning to end concerned with the last things. . . . [The petitions] "Hallowed be thy name," "thy kingdom come," and "thy will be done on earth as it is in heaven" entreat God to reveal his eschatological glory and usher in his everlasting reign. In the petition for bread, what is longed after is the heavenly manna, the bread of life, and the morrow is the great tomorrow, the consummation. "Forgive us our debts as we also have forgiven our debtors" is prayed in the face of the coming assize, when sins will be judged. And "do not put us to the test" refers to the coming time of trouble, to the messianic woes . . . to the final time of tribulation which will precede the renewal [so that here] one prays for preservation from evil or apostasy in the great tribulation (cf. Rev. 3:10).[51]

Thus, as Joachim Jeremias classically put this argument, in having his disciples pray the prayer, Jesus is urging the disciples to take advantage of the "privilege" they have as "sons/children of God," of "stretching forth their hands to grasp" in the present "the glory [and the gifts] of the [future] consummation."[52]

I have been arguing for a different understanding of this prayer. It was intended to shape the disciples as a group that, in word and deed,

---

Perrin (*The Kingdom of God in the Teaching of Jesus* [Philadelphia: Westminster, 1963], 197-98), G. R. Beasley-Murray (*Jesus and the Kingdom of God*, [Grand Rapids: Eerdmans, 1986]), and Donald A. Hagner (*Matthew 1-13*, Word Biblical Commentary [Dallas: Word, 1993]).

51. W. D. Davies and Dale C. Allison, *Matthew 1-7* (Edinburgh: T&T Clark, 1998), 594–95. See also Joachim Jeremias, *New Testament Theology: The Proclamation of Jesus* (New York: Scribner's, 1971), 193–203; Brown, "The Pater Noster," 276 and passim.

52. Joachim Jeremias, *Prayers of Jesus* [London: SCM, 1967], 104; and as already noted in previous chapters, Jeremias, *The Lord's Prayer* (Philadelphia: Fortress Press, 1964), 27.

would stand as a witness against the teachings of "this generation" regarding how Israel should be Israel. The occasion of Jesus' giving it to the disciples was his perception that they were in grave danger of falling away from their calling and becoming members of "this generation," and so he gave them the prayer as a means to secure from God the divine aid necessary to remain faithful to their calling. Its petitions echo the narrative of the wilderness generation, which Jesus regarded as the biblical prototype for the disobedient in his own time.

I shall turn next to examine how the petitions of the prayer work toward this end. In the course of that argument, it will be necessary also to spend some time examining the "eschatological" understanding of the prayer just sketched above, which stands today as the dominant alternative to the interpretation I am proposing.

5

Is the Disciples' Prayer an Eschatological Prayer?

In answering the question of whether the Disciples' Prayer is an eschatological prayer, I will proceed by having a close look at the arguments that supporters of the eschatological orientation employ to make their case. If those arguments seem not to carry weight, then the overall case for an eschatological reading of the prayer becomes wobbly, if not disproved.[1]

So what are these arguments? In the main, there are two. The first we've already noted: that the Disciples' Prayer is grounded in and derived from certain Jewish prayers—the Amidah, the Kaddish, and the Morning Prayer—which, so the argument goes, are themselves eschatological prayers in that they arise out of and express a heartfelt longing for the age of salvation long promised to Israel. These prayers are, on this view, centered on imploring God to bring about the

---

1. I follow here a procedure I first employed in "Matthew 6:9–13//Luke 11:2–4: An Eschatological Prayer?," *Biblical Theology Bulletin* 31 (2001): 96–105.

immediate arrival of that age and thus to bestow upon his faithful all of the end-time blessings that its arrival was expected to bring to them. The second argument is that the petitions themselves exhibit what the advocates of the eschatological view claim is a thoroughgoing "eschatological thrust," that is to say, a concern with the "last things."

We have already seen that the first argument is beset with formidable difficulties, the most important being our lack of knowledge of the earliest form and wording of the Amidah, the Kaddish, and the Morning Prayer, as well as doubts as to whether these prayers, whatever they originally said, were actually in any way contemporaneous with the Disciples' Prayer.[2] But for the sake of argument, let us set these difficulties aside; that is, let us assume not only that (1) the earliest form and wording of those prayers *can* be recovered and in fact has been recovered, but also that (2) in this wording there are parallels to that of the Disciples' Prayer, and that (3) the prayers *are* to be dated to early in the first century. The question then would be, is the focus and concern of these prayers the same as that reflected in the Disciples' Prayer? To answer that requires a prior question: What is the focus and concern of these prayers?

If we take our cue only from the petitions of the Amidah, the Kaddish, and the Morning Prayer noted above, as Jeremias and others seem to do, then the answer would appear to be: the wholly future kingdom or reign of God and the ardent hope that it might be

---

2. Both these and other difficulties in using these prayers as background to the Disciples' Prayer are roundly noted and acknowledged by John P. Meier (*A Marginal Jew*, vol. 2, *Mentor, Message, and Miracles* [New York: Doubleday, 1994], 297, 299, 361n36, 363n44). Indeed, it is because of these difficulties that Meier prescinds from taking the Amidah and the Kaddish directly into account in his exposition of the Disciples' Prayer. And yet, notably, Meier sneaks them in through the back door, so to speak, in that he believes they express part of a liturgical tradition that took shape before the first century of our era. See also Raymond E. Brown, "The Pater Noster as an Eschatological Prayer," in *New Testament Essays* (Garden City, NY: Doubleday, 1968), 281n20.

brought, ahead of its time, into the present. But once we take into account (1) the thrust of the liturgical setting in which the Kaddish was typically said; (2) what the eleventh petition in the Amidah and the "lead me not" petitions in the Morning Prayer follow on from; and (3) the frame of reference that these "contextualizations" give to these prayers, it becomes clear that they actually have another focus and concern, namely, securing divine aid to remain obedient in difficult times.

Consider, first, our passage from the Morning Prayer (Berakot 60b). The "lead us not" petition, which parallels Matt. 6:13 // Luke 11:4 is introduced by the call of the pious one for God to

> ... grant that my portion be your torah
> And accustom me [lit., make my custom] to the performance of [lit., to the hands of] [your] commandment.
> And prevent me from making my custom transgression.[3]

The parallel to Matt. 6:9 // Luke 11:2 in the Amidah is preceded and contextualized by a benediction that, according to Louis Finkelstein,[4] read as follows:

> 1. Blessed are you Lord God of our Fathers: God of Abraham, God of Isaac and God of Jacob; a God great, mighty and revered; the God Most High, Master of heaven and earth.
> —Blessed are you Lord the Shield of Abraham.
>
> 2. Mighty are you who sustain the living and revive the dead.
> —Blessed are you Lord, who revive the dead.

---

3. "Babylonian Talmud: Tractate Berakoth," trans. Maurice Simon, *Come and Hear* website, http://www.come-and-hear.com/berakoth/berakoth_60.html#PARTb. A second version of the prayer has here:
   > That [you may] accustom me to study [the practice of] your torah
   > and [may you] cause me to cleave to your commandments."
   ("Baylonian Talmud Masechet Berachot," *Congregation Emanu-el* website, http://www.emanuelsf.org/document.doc?id=170)
4. Louis Finkelstein, "The Development of Amidah," *Jewish Quarterly Review* n.s. 16 (1925): 1–43, 127–70.

> 3. Holy are you and revered is your Name and there is no God beside you.
> —Blessed are you Lord, Holy God.

There follow specific petitions, which also precede the petition paralleled in the Disciples' Prayer:

> 4. Our Father (Abinu), grant us knowledge and understanding and awareness of you.
> —Blessed are you Lord, who grant knowledge.
>
> 5. Our Father, bring us back to your Torah and return us in perfect repentance to you Presence.
> —Blessed are you Lord, who delight in repentance.

When the Kaddish was recited liturgically, this was apparently done only after, and therefore within the context of thought provided by, the recitation of the Amidah and, more importantly, of the Shema, the confession of faith derived from Deut. 6:4. The Shema both calls the people of Israel to love God with their whole of heart, soul, and mind, and warns them sternly against "forgetting" their covenant obligations to God, refusing to trust in him and his ways, and putting him to the test (see Deut. 6:12, 16).[5]

It would seem, then, that if the Disciples' Prayer were indeed somehow grounded in these prayers and did derive its focus and concern from theirs, then we should identify that focus and concern not as the future coming of God's kingdom but as preservation in faithfulness and avoidance of apostasy.

What about the second argument, that the thrust of each of the requests in the Disciples' prayer is itself eschatological?

---

5. As John Nolland notes (*The Gospel of Matthew*, New International Greek Testament Commentary [Grand Rapids: Eerdmans, 2005], 286, attempts to read the first petition of the Kaddish as eschatological in orientation are unconvincing since the prayer is ethically motivated, and, in line with Isa. 29:23 and 1 Enoch 61:12, calls on God's people to glorify God by actions.

I begin with the "kingdom" request (ἐλθέτω ἡ βασιλεία σου [elthetō hē basileia sou] [Matt. 6:10a // Luke 11:2c]) since this is the request that, as the "eschatologists" themselves note (as I will call the advocates of the purely eschatological interpretation), has served as the cornerstone of their view that the Disciples' Prayer is a prayer that "prays down" into the present the expected glory of the end of the ages as described in Jewish eschatological texts. I will turn subsequently to examine the request not to be "led into" πειρασμός (peirasmos).

The "Kingdom" Request

Surely, the eschatologists argue, given the import of the request's language, especially in its use of the aorist imperative form of the verb "to come," which makes the "kingdom" petition a call for a once-only event that affects all history,[6] and given its formal parallelism with those in the Amidah and the Kaddish that have eschatological intent, the request that God's reign (βασιλεία) should "come" stands self-evidently as conclusive proof that the Disciples' Prayer is an eschatological prayer. Is it not obvious that what we have here is a plea for God to act now, to do something he was expected to do only in the future, namely, establish decisively his sovereignty on earth?

Well, no: it is not self-evident, and for several reasons. First, as both Buist Fanning and Stanley Porter have shown, the aorist imperative in a request (here, "may it come") does not signify asking for something that is to happen "once only"; it indicates only that something specific should happen in a specific situation.[7]

---

6. See Brown, "Pater Noster," 292.
7. Buist M. Fanning, *Verbal Aspect in New Testament Greek* (Oxford: Clarendon, 1990), 97, 380–82; Stanley Porter, *Verbal Aspect in the Greek of the New Testament, with Reference to Tense and Mood* (New York: Peter Lang, 1989), 347–50.

Second, as my teacher George Caird has noted, the eschatological interpretation of the petition assumes, following what Ronald Knox called "the token word fallacy" in which words become a kind of coinage with a uniform and invariable rate of exchange,[8] that what Jesus meant by βασιλεία had to be what the term was taken to mean elsewhere in contemporary Judaism. But if the Synoptic evangelists are right in their insistence that Jesus spent much of his time explaining what the kingdom of God was, would it not follow that he did not mean what everybody else meant by it?[9] (see, e.g., Mark 4:26-29; Matt. 13:24-30; Matt. 13:31-32 // Mark 4:30-32 // Luke 13:18-19; Matt. 13:33 // Luke 13:20-21; Matt. 13:44-46, 47-50).

Third, to say that the petition is a plea for God soon to usher in his βασιλεία implies not only that at the time the prayer was given Jesus believed that God had not yet done so but also that God had no intention of doing so, at least in the foreseeable future, and thus had to be implored to do so. Nothing is more certain, however, in both Matthew and Luke's (and Mark's) portraits of Jesus than that Jesus knew God's kingdom to be a powerfully imminent, if not an already present, reality. Indeed, in the contexts in the Gospels of Matthew and Luke in which the giving of the Disciples' Prayer takes place, the prevailing assumption about God's βασιλεία is that it, and the opportunity it offers for the salvation of God's people, have already arrived (see Matt. 4:16; Luke 4:16-21; 19:44). In the light of this, it seems unlikely that the petition in Matt. 6:10a // Luke 11:2c is a plea for God to act now to do something he was expected to do only in the (distant?) future. Why urge anyone to pray for the accomplishment of a fait accompli?

Third, as already observed in chapter 3, the wording of petitions in Jewish prayers wherein God is clearly urged to bring about the

---

8. R. Knox, *On Englishing the Bible* (London, 1949) 11.
9. Caird, *New Testament Theology*, 367. See too, Crump, *Knocking*, 122.

early dawning of his βασιλεία is different from the language in Matt. 6:10a // Luke 11:2c. As these Jewish prayers evince, the standard practice when invoking God with regard to his kingly rule was by use of the imperative "reign," spoken to God ("You yourself reign over us"), or the indirect (passive) construction "may your kingdom be revealed" (or manifested). The expression in the Disciples' Prayer, using the verb "to come," is so scarce (appearing only in Mic. 4:8) as to appear unparalleled in Jewish prayer—a point that a number of the eschatologists themselves concede.[10] Further, neither of the forms just cited clearly presupposes the absence or remoteness of God's reign, which a thoroughly eschatological understanding would require.

Further, when we compare the petition in the Disciples' Prayer to other prayer petitions in early Judaism and the early Jesus movement as well, we observe connotations that go beyond a simple request for the arrival now of a future reality. Four observations bear consideration here. First, recall that, as we have just seen, the petition is set by both Matthew and Luke in the context of Jesus' larger proclamation not only that the kingdom has arrived but that both those who seek the kingdom and those who think they have it as their heritage must turn and conform themselves to its demands if it is ever to be theirs.[11] With this as its immediate background, ἐλθέτω ἡ βασιλεία might be regarded as resembling the calls in rabbinic literature for Israel to seek God's aid to be conformed to charity, obedience, justice, and repentance in order to be rendered worthy of the deliverance that was faithful Israel's inheritance.[12]

---

10. Meier, *Mentor, Message, and Miracles*, 298; W. D. Davies and Dale C. Allison, *Matthew 1–7* (Edinburgh: T&T Clark, 1998), 604; see also Bruce Chilton, *Jesus' Prayer and Jesus' Eucharist: His Personal Practice of Spirituality* (Edinburgh: Trinity Press International, 1997), 37. Meier even declares the occurrence in Mic. 4:8 irrelevant (*Mentor, Message, and Miracles*, 362n39).
11. Note, too, that in Matthew's Gospel, the prayer follows the second of three pithy sayings on "doing righteousness." So Hans Dieter Betz, *The Sermon on the Mount: A Commentary on the Sermon on the Mount, Including the Sermon on the Plain (Matthew 5:3–7:27 and Luke 6:20-49)*, ed. Adela Yarbro Collins, Hermeneia (Minneapolis: Fortress Press, 1995), 349.

Second, consider the fact, again noted by George Caird, that in the formal and material parallel to the "kingdom" request found in Rev. 22:20c—namely, the petition ἔρχου, κύριε Ἰησοῦ (*erchou, kyrie Iēsou*), which, like the "kingdom" request in the Disciples' Prayer, consists of a form of ἔρχομαι (*erchomai*) in the imperative subject, and also is uttered in the context of an announcement of the dawning of a divine visitation.[13] The function of the verb ἔρχομαι is not so much to express a sense of distance and separation as it is to invite closeness, and concomitantly to express the desire to be acceptable to the one invited to "come." It is not the Lord (or, in the Disciples' Prayer, the kingdom) that must be "turned" so that it "come"; rather, both prayers express the desire that the one praying be turned from disobedience and conformed to the reality, or the person, that is called upon to "come."[14] This suggests that the ἐλθέτω in the petition ἐλθέτω ἡ βασιλεία σου expresses the wish to be made worthy of God's kingdom and to be protected from all that would prevent this end.

Third, as Brant Pitre has noted, in Mic. 4:8 the "kingdom" that is to "come" is a people, not a "reign" or a territory, and more particularly,

---

12. See, e.g., Baba Batra 10a: "It has been taught: R. Judah says: Great is charity, in that it brings the redemption nearer, as it says, Thus saith the Lord, Keep ye judgment and do righteousness [*zedakah*], for my salvation is near to come and my righteousness to be revealed (Isa. 56:1)." And Yoma 86b: "R. Jonathan said: Great is repentance, because it brings about redemption, as it is said And a redeemer will come to Zion, and unto them that turn from transgression in Jacob, i.e., why will a redeemer come to Zion? Because of those that turn from transgression in Jacob." On this, see G. F. Moore, *Judaism in the First Centuries of the Christian Era* (Cambridge: Harvard University Press, 1927), 2:350–52.
13. See Rev. 22:20ab: "He who testifies to these things says, 'Surely I am coming soon.'" Cf. Matt. 4:17; Luke 4:16-21).
14. According to Caird (*The Revelation of St. John the Divine* [London: Black, 1966], 288), Rev. 22:20c is "a prayer that Christ will come again to win *in his faithful servant* the victory which is both Calvary and Armageddon. It is the prayer which says. 'All I ask is to know Christ and the power of his resurrection, to share his sufferings and conform to the pattern of his death, if only I may arrive at the resurrection of the dead (Phil. iii. 10-11). It is a prayer that the Christian, confronted by the great ordeal, may 'endure as one who sees the invisible' (Heb. xi. 27), and may hear above the harsh sentence of the Roman judge the triumph song of heaven" (emphasis added).

it is a people called and enabled by God to be his holy remnant, his faithful representatives on earth.[15]

Finally, consider the implication of the fact that Jesus uses the phrase ἐλθέτω ἡ βασιλεία σου as a coordinate of the phrase "May your will be done on earth as it is in heaven" (γενηθήτω τὸ θέλημά σου, ὡς ἐν οὐρανῷ καὶ ἐπὶ γῆς [*genēthētō to thelēma sou, hōs en ouranō kai epi gēs*], Matt. 6:10bc). If we assume, as I think we should, that the concern of this coordinate phrase is God's enabling of the disciples' obedience in the face of a desire to act otherwise,[16] then it seems more likely that the sense of the petition ἐλθέτω ἡ βασιλεία σου, for Jesus (and certainly for Matthew), was less to implore God to manifest his reign ahead of the time he intended to do so, than to invite God to ensure that the will of his people is in harmony with his own purposes for them. The fuller connotation of the petition might then be paraphrased, "may we be made worthy of your reign by being conformed not to our own will but to yours."

One can hardly say, in the light of all this, that the eschatological interpretation of the "kingdom" request in the Disciples' Prayer has been proved impossible; but the preceding arguments should at least make clear that it is not inevitable or self-evident. Indeed, insofar as it must fly against other evidence in the Gospels regarding Jesus' view of the kingdom as imminent or already present, the eschatological understanding of the petition as "praying down" into the present the benefits of a future kingdom seems forced. Indeed, the evidence shows that rather than its being an imploration to God to make his kingdom arrive, ἐλθέτω ἡ βασιλεία σου is actually a plea for divine aid for the obedience that renders one worthy of that kingdom, and against apostasy.[17]

---

15. Brant Pitre, "The Lord's Prayer and the New Exodus," *Letter & Spirit* 2 (2006): 83.
16. The conformity of this phrase with the Matthean version of Jesus' prayer in Gethsemane, where God's enabling of obedience in the face of a desire to be otherwise is exactly what is asked for, makes the ethical interpretation of Matt. 6:10bc certain.

The significance of this conclusion must not be underestimated. Since the very petition the eschatologists employ as the cornerstone of their interpretation of the focus and concern of the Disciples' Prayer does not bear the weight placed on it, but instead points in another direction entirely, then the case for a purely eschatological understanding of the prayer looks far less certain than it has often been thought to be.

But this objection may not be fatal if the other requests in the Disciples' Prayer have an eschatological orientation. So let us turn to the next petition that has been thought to bear such an orientation.

The "Name" Request

We have seen above that eschatologists take this request to be a plea for God to do in the present what, according to their reading of apocalyptic speculation, he was expected to do in the future, namely, manifest himself finally and decisively to all the world in all his transcendent power. It is, as Raymond E. Brown notes, "a prayer that God accomplish the ultimate sanctification of His name, the complete manifestation of His holiness, the last of His salvific acts";[18] as Joachim Jeremias put it, an "entreaty for the revelation of God's eschatological kingdom."[19]

Now, as we endeavor to determine whether the "name" request, which is set out in a passive formulation, may legitimately be characterized in such eschatological terms, it is important to note that in both the Hebrew Bible and Second Temple (or Formative)

---

17. I note with interest that this is also the meaning of the petition "May your Holy Spirit come upon us and cleanse us," which apparently Marcion and Gregory of Nyssa found in place of "May your kingdom come" in their texts of Luke 11:2. If we could be sure that the variant was an intentional substitution for what most scholars consider to be the original Lukan text of Luke 11:2, then we would have even more evidence than we now have that the kingdom petition was seen in the early church as having an ethical, and not an eschatological meaning.
18. Brown, "Pater Noster," 292.
19. Jeremias, *The Lord's Prayer*, 21.

Judaism the "sanctification of God's name" was not thought of as activity that *only* God could engage in. Human beings (and corporately, Israel) could also "hallow the name of God." Moreover, this activity signified two different things depending on who was denoted as engaged in it. God's sanctifying his name signified his seeing to it that he is finally recognized by all the world for who and what he is by manifesting himself through a powerful intervention on behalf of his people Israel, which would liberate them from oppression by their enemies.[20] Human action (or action on the part of Israel) to sanctify God's name entailed their willingness to adopt a posture of faithfulness to God's ways and of trust in his promises, especially in times of hardship or trial, even to the point of becoming a martyr for God's cause.[21] Note the import of the statement attributed by Rabbi Jose (b. Halaphta) to the popular model of piety Phineas, who when he placed himself in grave danger to preserve the holiness of God justified his action by declaring, "If the horse risks itself on the day of battle and is ready to dies for its master, ought I not to do the same for the holiness of the name of God?"[22]

---

20. Whether this entailed God's bringing an actual end to the present sinful world is, as we shall see, by no means certain.
21. Ulrich Luz, *Matthew 1–7*, Hermeneia (Minneapolis: Fortress Press, 2007), 317, who cites the data in Hermann L. Strack and Paul Billerbeck, *Kommentar Zum Neuen Testament Aus Talmud Und Midrasch* (Munich: Beck, 1922), 1:411–18. So also B. Young, *The Jewish Background of the Lord's Prayer* (Austin, TX: Center for Judaic Christian Studies, 1984), 8–9; Reuven Hammer, *Entering Jewish Prayer: A Guide to Personal Devotion and the Worship Service* (New York: Schocken, 1994) 282. As W. Gunther Plaut and David E. Stein note, "The concept of hallowing the name was transformed in formative Judaism into a powerful moral challenge. The prestige of Israel's God among the Gentiles—the Rabbis taught—is not God's worry, it is humankind's responsibility. Jews must so live and act as to win for their God the respect of all mankind. Any behavior that brings public disgrace on Jews and Judaism is *hillul haShem*, profanation of the divine Name; any action that enhances the dignity and honor of Judaism, among which being willing to give up one's life in a time of persecution rather than abandoning one's obedience to God is exemplary, is *kiddush haShem*, sanctification of the Name. . . . The highest act of kiddush ha-shem is to die for one's faith" (*The Torah: A Modern Commentary* [New York: URJ Press, 2005], 808.
22. Exodus Rabbah 33:5. Quoted in Martin Hengel, *The Zealots: Studies on the Jewish Freedom Movement from the time of Herod I to 70 CE* (Edinburgh: T&T Clark, 1989), 158.

Why is this observation important? Because it means that for the request "Father, let your name be hallowed" to have the orientation that the eschatologists claim it has, the one envisioned within the petition as the "hallower of God's name" must be God; furthermore, God must be envisioned as doing so only by ending history. Absent this, the case for the eschatological orientation of the "name" request collapses.

That it is indeed God and not human beings whom Jesus envisioned as the agent of the sought-after sanctification of God's name has been argued on two grounds. First, the request is set not only in a passive voice formulation but also in a particular kind of passive-voice formulation known as a "divine passive,"[23] that is to say, a way of speaking about God as agent without using the divine name. We find Jesus using just such a formulation elsewhere in the Beatitudes. Second, the language of the request as a whole is grounded in, and is meant to evoke, Ezek. 36:23-27, which speaks of God acting to sanctify himself and his name.[24]

Now while it is true that the verb employed in the "name" request, ἁγιάζω (*hagiazō* = "make holy, consecrate, sanctify"), is in the passive voice (the aorist passive imperative, to be exact), I doubt it is meant as a "divine passive." In the first place, as the history of exegesis shows, until the dawning of the eschatological interpretation of the Disciples' Prayer, no one thought to read the verb in any way other than as a true passive, the implied subject of which was the disciples (i.e., "may your name be hallowed" by the disciples). Grammatically there is nothing to indicate that it should be taken in any other way, since the aorist passive imperative in a petition conforms to Greek

---

23. Davies and Allison, *Matthew 1–7*, 602; Eduard Schweizer, *The Gospel According to Matthew* (Atlanta: John Knox, 1975), 151; Joachim Jeremias, *New Testament Theology: The Proclamation of Jesus* (New York: Scribner's, 1971), 11.
24. Meier, *Mentor, Message, and Miracles*, 295–98.

prayer style in general where the pray-er is the subject of the verb.²⁵ One suspects, then, that the claim that the verb is an instance of the divine passive is an instance of special pleading, grounded in circular logic and dictated by the need to find evidence to support a prior conclusion. In the second place, the use of the divine passive would be out of keeping with the tone of the prayer, where the wish to avoid speaking of or addressing God directly seems to have no part, as the direct address to God in the opening of the prayer clearly shows. In the third place, in the parallels to Matt. 6:9 // Luke 11:2 found in such Jewish prayers as the Kaddish, the expression equivalent to "let your name be hallowed," namely, "May his Great name be magnified and hallowed in the world which he has created according to his will," includes no divine passive. Rather, the idea expressed there is that of the sanctifying of God's name by Israel.²⁶

While as I said above the language appears to evoke Ezek. 36:23-27—indeed, so much so that I grant that what the petition asks for is what is described in those verses—it does not follow that the petition envisions God, rather than human beings, as the presumed "hallower" of his name, let alone that God should do so by bringing about some final judgment (as the eschatological interpretation implies). For the theme of the Ezekiel passage is how God's name will be hallowed *by Israel* through God's enabling them to be faithful and obedient during, and in response to, an earthly, historical crisis. Consider the following points:

1. In the larger context in which these verses appear, God is portrayed as angry with Israel, his covenant partner, for

---

25. On this, see Friedrich Blass, Albert Debrunner, and Robert W. Funk, *A Greek Grammar of the New Testament and Other Early Christian Literature* (Chicago: University of Chicago Press, 1961), sec. 337 (4); Luz, *Matthew 1–7*, 316, who cites Eduard Schweizer, *Griechische Grammatik*, 5th ed. (Munich: Beck, 1977), 2:341.
26. Luz, *Matthew 1–7*, 379.

"profaning" his name at a particular time in history. As Ezek. 36:20-21 relate: "But when they came to the nations, wherever they came, they profaned my holy name.... But I had concern for my holy name, which the house of Israel caused to be profaned among the nations to which they came" (cf. v. 23). And so God "scattered them among the nations, and they were dispersed through the countries" (v. 19a).

2. As verse 20 shows, this "profaning God's name" (ἐβεβήλωσαν τὸ ὄνομά μου τὸ ἅγιον [*ebebēlōsan to onoma mou to hagion*]) is identified as the dishonor brought on God when, after God had sent Israel into exile and deprived them of their land, people not of Israel charged that God had betrayed his stated promises to be Israel's protector and had no interest in his elect: "They profaned my holy name, in that men said of them, 'These are the people of the Lord, and yet they had to go out of his land.'"

3. As verses 17-20 show, this profanation of the name was ultimately rooted in Israel's refusal to obey God and to remain faithful to their covenant obligations when Israel "came to the nations," that is, from the moment they entered into the land that God had promised them.

> When the house of Israel dwelt in their own land, they defiled it by their ways and their doings; their conduct before me was like the uncleanness of a woman in her impurity. So I poured out my wrath upon them for the blood which they had shed in the land, for the idols with which they had defiled it. I scattered them among the nations, and they were dispersed through the countries; in accordance with their conduct and their deeds I judged them.

4. As verses 23-28 show, to vindicate the holiness of his name, God promises to move decisively in history, not at its end, not only to restore the house of Israel to its land (vv. 23-24), but also to make it so that he will never again have to remove Israel from it

as he once did, by ensuring that immediately after the exile Israel will never again engage in apostasy.

> A new heart I will give you, and a new spirit I will put within you; and I will take out of your flesh the heart of stone and give you a heart of flesh. And I will put my spirit within you, and cause you to walk in my statutes and be careful to observe my ordinances. You shall dwell in the land which I gave to your fathers; and you shall be my people, and I will be your God. (vv. 26-28)

It follows from these observations that if the "name" request is meant so to evoke Ezek. 36:23-27 that the petition is meant to ask for what is described in those verses, then the "name" request is not for God himself to sanctify his name by *any* action, let alone an eschatological one, that is independent of human behavior. Rather, it is for him to act as he said he would and prevent his elect from dishonoring him now, at the time the petition is uttered, by being disobedient to what he asks of them.

In any case, the idea that God is the implied agent of the passive verb ἁγιασθήτω (*hagiastētō*) in Matt. 6:9c // Luke 11:2 is ruled out for two other reasons. First, there is the often overlooked implication of what it means to ask God to ensure that his name "be hallowed." Logically, the petition ἁγιασθήτω τὸ ὄνομά σου, "[Please, God,] make it so that your name is hallowed," also implies a negative petition, a prohibition of its opposite: "[Please, God], make it so that your name is not profaned." Thus whoever is envisioned as the agent of "hallowing" must also have both the ability and the inclination to "profane" God's name. This consideration, then, would seem to rule out God as the envisaged actor. God cannot profane his own name. It also rules out the nations, or those not of Israel, since hallowing and profaning are actions that can be undertaken only by those who are covenanted with God (as Ezekiel 36 testifies!). So we are left with those who are viewed in the prayer as having the right to call God

"Father," that is, those who are covenantally related to him, and those whom God proclaims as his "sons." The only ones who qualify here are the disciples.

Second, if in the "name" request God were envisioned as the subject of ἁγιασθήτω, then Jesus would appear to be telling his disciples to pray for the realization of the very antithesis of his ministry. For in the Hebrew Bible and in Formative Judaism, the end result of God sanctifying or hallowing his name is the redemption of sinful Israel through the destruction of those who traditionally have oppressed her.[27] But the destruction of Israel's enemies is hardly what Jesus countenances or envisions as the goal of his ministry, let alone anything he wishes his disciples to pray for or be a part of.

In addition to all of this, there is one further consideration. As Gustaf Dalman and others have pointed out, in Jesus' time and afterward, to pray that God's name be hallowed was to pray for divine aid to follow his commandments faithfully, especially in times of crises, even should that be at the price of one's own life.[28]

So what can we conclude in the light of these observations? First, there is no reason to see the "name" request as having an eschatological thrust. Second, the request is a plea that the disciples might be enabled to show themselves as faithful servants of God.

---

27. As is seemingly admitted by Meier (*Mentor, Message, and Miracles*, 299) when he, taking God as the subject of ἁγιασθήτω, claims that what is besought in Matt. 6:9c // Luke 11:2 is God's bringing "about a definitive manifestation of his power, glory, and holiness by defeating the Gentiles, gathering the scattered tribes of Israel back to the holy land, and establishing his divine rule fully and forever."
28. Gustaf Dalman, *Jesus—Jeshua: Studies in the Gospels* (1929; repr., Eugene, OR: Wipf & Stock, 2005), 212–14. See also David Crump, *Knocking on Heaven's Door: A New Testament Theology of Petitionary Prayer* (Grand Rapids: Baker Academic, 2006), 119. This idea certainly lies behind the statements of Jesus about how his death on the cross shows God's glory (see John 17) as well as how Peter would glorify God through the martyrdom he would experience as a result of following Jesus (John 21:19).

The "Bread" Request

As we have seen above, eschatologists claim that the request for bread in the Disciples' Prayer expresses a longing not for ordinary bread but for the heavenly manna, the bread of life, which, according to them, was in Jewish eschatological thought a gift God was expected to give to his people at the dawning of his age of salvation. They buttress this view by noting two things: First, that the (notoriously difficult) expression τὸν ἄρτον ἡμων τὸν ἐπιούσιον (*ton arton hēmōn ton epiousion*) in the petition (which is usually rendered "our daily bread") is best taken as a reference to the "manna" that was once distributed by God to the wilderness generation and which Jews of Jesus' day expected to come down again from heaven in the end times. This argument is based on such texts as Syrian Apocalypse of Baruch 29:8 ("And it will happen at that time that the treasury of manna will come down again from on high, and they will eat of it in those years because these are they who have arrived at the consummation of time"); Sibylline Oracles, fr. 3, 49; Rev. 2:17 ("Whoever has ears, let them hear what the Spirit says to the churches. To the one who is victorious, I will give some of the hidden manna"); and Qoheleth Rabbah (a midrash on Ecclesiastes) 1 on Eccles. 1:9 ("As the first redeemer caused manna to come down, so will the last"). Second, the eschatological interpreters contend that behind the initial wording of the request (in which the verb "to give" is set out as an imperative) stands a profound sense of not having whatever τὸν ἄρτον ἡμῶν τὸν ἐπιούσιον is, and feeling a great physical or temporal need for it.

How valid are these claims? The first—that Jews believed God would distribute bread in the end times—is highly questionable. The Sibylline Oracles, fr., 3, 49, and Qoheleth Rabbah 1 are late.[29] We do not know whether what the author of the Apocalypse of Baruch says

THE DISCIPLES' PRAYER

in this regard—presumably as a word of consolation to Palestinian Jews who survived the Jewish War, given that his work is apparently written as a response to the fall of the Jerusalem temple[30]—is a belief that is peculiar to himself and not widely known.[31] So these texts are unreliable as witnesses in Jesus' day to what was and what was not part of any Jewish scenarios of the "last days." Revelation 2:17 does not speak of a bread that will be revealed in the end times; rather, the "manna" spoken of there is what was intended by God from the beginning of creation to prosper Israel in times of testing.[32]

What of the validity of the second claim? I accept the eschatologists' view that whatever the expression τὸν ἄρτον ἡμῶν τὸν ἐπιούσιον means (whether "bread of necessity," "bread for today," "bread for the morrow," or "ration of bread"), it is, as Tertullian recognized so long ago,[33] at base clearly a reference to the

---

29. Our fragment from the oracles may be as late as the seventh century CE. Qoheleth Rabbah is post-talmudic.
30. On this, see George W. E. Nickelsburg, *Jewish Literature between the Bible and the Mishnah* (Minneapolis: Fortress Press, 2011), 283.
31. Extremely pertinent here is a remark by N. T. Wright on the knowledge among Jews of Jesus' day of what was asserted in apocalyptic literature such as the Apocalypse of Baruch: "'Apocalyptic' is a type of literature which was both available to all in principle as one way of saying things that might be difficult to say otherwise, and most likely cherished and read, in the case of individual writings, by a comparatively small group. That is, any Jew might read, say, *1 Enoch*, and might find there meanings of which he or she could approve; but the chances are that most Jews, including many who cherished wild dreams about the future, did not in fact know most of the works now collected in Charlesworth's *Pseudepigrapha* [the most recent collection of noncanonical apocalyptic Jewish literature written between 200 BCE and 600 CE] and that many Jews, if they had come across such literature, would have regarded it with great suspicion. That is why one cannot base an account of Judaism on such writings, but must always start at least with the things we know to have been common to all Jews." (*The New Testament and the People of God*, Christian Origins and the Question of God 1 [Minneapolis: Fortress Press, 1992], 208.)
32. On this, see G. K. Beale, *The Book of Revelation: A Commentary on the Greek Text*, New International Greek Testament Commentary (Grand Rapids: Eerdmans, 1999), 251. See, too, David Aune (*Revelation 1–5*, Word Biblical Commentary [Dallas: Word, 1997], 189), who notes not only that the adjectival participle το κεκρυμμένου, "hidden," means belonging to those who are faithful to God, but also that the point of the metaphor is to assert that "victorious Christians will be rewarded with eternal life in which intimate fellowship with God will be enjoyed."
33. Tertullian, *Against Marcion* 4.26.4.

manna from heaven given by God each day and for the morrow for the sustenance of Israel during their trials in their wilderness wanderings.[34] It is surely not ordinary bread that is being asked for. It is "our" bread—a bread that, in the wider context of the prayer and the sermon in which it is embedded, belongs only to υἱοὶ θεοῦ.[35] But—and here's the rub—we have no clear reason to believe that the aim of the request is for the satisfaction of a felt need, and that functionally the request itself is a plea to gain something that is lacking. Several considerations are relevant here.

First of all, none of the other petitions in the Disciples' Prayer, and especially the other so-called "we" petitions found there, have as their focus the remedy of a need. This is clear even where it appears not to be the case, that is, in the forgiveness request at Matt. 6:12 // Luke 11:4a, which at first glance seems to presuppose an awareness on the disciples' part of a profound need to be forgiven by God of their "sins." But given that the request is followed by a clause that functions to give the reason why (in Jesus' eyes) the disciples can call on God for "forgiveness," the awareness presupposed in Matt. 6:12//

---

34. See W. Foerster, "ἐπιούσιος," in *Theological Dictionary of the New Testament*, ed. Gerhard Kittel and Gerhard Friedrich, trans. Geoffrey W. Bromiley (Grand Rapids: Eerdmans, 1964), 2:597; J. Carmignac, *Recherches sur le "Nôtre Père"* (Paris: Letouzay & Anè, 1969), 190; A. Vögtle, "Der 'eschatologische' Bezug der Wir Bitten des Vaterunser," in *Jesus and Paulus: Festschrift für W. G. Kummel*, eds. E. E. Ellis and E. Grässer (Vandenhoeck & Ruprecht: Göttingen, 1976), 348–50; Davies and Allison, *Matthew 1–7*, 607–9. For an extensive review and analysis of the other possible meanings and referents of τὸν ἄρτον [ἡμῶν] τὸν ἐπιούσιον, see Foerster, "ἐπιούσιος," 590–99.
35. The fact that the bread spoken of in the request is specifically a special bread, the bread belonging to the disciples as God's υἱοί (though note that according to Adolf von Harnack [*Marcion: Das Evangelium vom fremden Gott; Eine Monographie zur Geschichte der Grundlegung der katholischen Kirche* (Leipzig: Hinrichs, 1924), 207] Marcion reads τὸν ἄρτον σου ["your [i.e., God's] bread"] instead of τὸν ἄρτον ἡμῶν ["our [i.e., the disciples'] bread"]), seems to me to rule out any notion, recently argued for by Crossan and especially by Douglas Oakman (*The Political Aims of Jesus* [Minneapolis: Fortress Press, 2012]), that what is asked for in this request is what all people in an agrarian society, where nourishment for the following day could not simply be taken for granted, regarded as a daily necessity. It also rules out nourishment of all of humankind's physical needs, as many sermons and devotional commentaries on the Disciples' Prayer claim.

Luke 11:4a on the part of the disciples is not that they have offended God and are therefore in desperate need of his mercies, but that they are presently in good standing with him, having been faithful to what he has bidden them do to show themselves actually to be, his υἱοὶ. Why, then, would the bread petition have the remedy of a need as its focus?

Second, as Hans Dieter Betz,[36] W. Foerster,[37] Rick Byargeon,[38] and even such prominent eschatologists as Davies and Allison[39] have acknowledged, the closest parallel to, and possible source for, the "bread" request is the "bread" petition in Prov. 30.8-9 ("keep feeding me with my apportioned bread" רֵאשׁ וָעֹשֶׁר אַל־תִּתֶּן־לִי הַטְרִיפֵנִי לֶחֶם חֻקִּי). However, as its context shows, it is not set against, nor does it arise out of, a perceived lack or absence of its object. On the contrary, it assumes the provision by God of the bread. Moreover, the sense of that prayer is that the petitioner wishes to be satisfied with what God provides *rather than* seeking other "breads"; it is an expression of confidence in God to provide for his people

Third, the imperative used in the petition does not require, as is usually supposed, that the bread be something those uttering the petition do not already have. Quite the opposite, the imperative shows that this bread is envisaged as something that was previously and continuously given to the pray-ers prior to their uttering the petition and as something they now already have in their possession. This is most evident in the Lukan form of the petition, which uses the present-tense imperative form διδοῦ (*didou*; from δίδωμι [*didōmi*], "give"), which gives the petition the sense of a plea that God not stop his provision of the "daily bread" that he has been providing his

---

36. *Sermon on the Mount*, 398.
37. "Ἐπιούσιος", TDNT 2, 598.
38. "Echoes of Wisdom in the Lord's Prayer (Matt 6:9-13)", *JETS* 41 (1998) 353-365, esp. 357-362.
39. *Matthew 1-7*, 606.

faithful (the present imperative bears the meaning "keep on giving"). This continuous sense is also implicit in Matthew's use of the aorist active imperative δὸς, which might be rendered, "do give."

Finally, and perhaps most importantly, consider that if Jesus were in fact urging his disciples to utter the sort of plea that the eschatologists believe the "bread" request to be, he would be contradicting his express teaching that his disciples not be anxious about obtaining the necessities of life (Matt. 6:25-34):

> Therefore I tell you, do not worry about your life, what you will eat or drink; or about your body, what you will wear. Is not life more important than food, and the body more important than clothes? Look at the birds of the air; they do not sow or reap or store away in barns, and yet your heavenly Father feeds them. Are you not much more valuable than they? Who of you by worrying can add a single hour to his life? And why do you worry about clothes? See how the lilies of the field grow. They do not labor or spin. Yet I tell you that not even Solomon in all his splendor was dressed like one of these. If that is how God clothes the grass of the field, which is here today and tomorrow is thrown into the fire, will he not much more clothe you, O you of little faith? So do not worry, saying, "What shall we eat?" or "What shall we drink?" or "What shall we wear?" For the pagans run after all these things, and your heavenly Father knows that you need them. But seek first his kingdom and his righteousness, and all these things will be given to you as well. Therefore do not worry about tomorrow, for tomorrow will worry about itself. Each day has enough trouble of its own. (cf. Luke 12:22-31)

He would also be contradicting his teaching on the certainty of God's fatherly care for his faithful.

> Which of you, if his son asks for bread, will give him a stone? Or if he asks for a fish, will give him a snake? If you, then, though you are evil, know how to give good gifts to your children, how much more will your Father in heaven give good gifts to those who ask him! (Matt. 7:9-11. Cf. Luke 11:11-13.)

In the light all of this, we have little reason to think that the petition assumes a lack of what is prayed for. Nor have we reason to think that it is a plea to God to overcome this lack.[40] On the contrary, the evidence indicates that the petition assumes the contrary.

The Forgiveness Request

According to the eschatologists, the horizon of this request is not daily or ordinary life but the great reckoning Jesus saw as fast approaching, the imminent "disclosure of God's majesty in the final judgment."[41] It is grounded, the argument goes, in a consciousness on Jesus' part that the disciples are involved in sin and debt, and that only God's gracious forgiveness can save them from the wrath to come. So, in "anticipation of [this] judgment, they utter a petition for a complete forgiveness of sin."[42]

The eschatological interpreters are led to this conclusion by several considerations. The first is that there was an expectation of a coming judgment for sinners within second-Temple Judaism. The second is the notion that if the request was not eschatological in orientation, it would be out of place in the midst of all the other requests in the Disciples' Prayer which are (on their view) eschatologically orientated.[43] The third is that the form of the verbs used in the request—the aorist, which is thought to indicate a kind of once for all-ness rather than a continuing action—is taken to indicate that the forgiveness requested is viewed as a one-time event, the expression "forgive us our sins" being taken to mean "forgive us this once" rather than a process or a series of repeated actions.[44] And fourth, it

---

40. Notably, this would remain the case even should the eschatologists be correct in their claim that Jews expected God to give bread to his people when the "last days" arrived.
41. Joachim Jeremias, *The Lord's Prayer* (Philadelphia: Fortress Press, 1964), 27.
42. Brown, "Pater Noster," 310.
43. Ibid., 309; Davies and Allison, *Matthew 1–7*, 612.
44. Brown, "Pater Noster," 308. But notably not by Meier, *Marginal Jew*, 2:368n38.

is supported, they suppose, by the teaching of Jesus on forgiveness at Matthew 5:23-25:

> So when you are offering your gift at the altar, if you remember that your brother or sister has something against you, leave your gift there before the altar and go; first be reconciled to your brother or sister, and then come and offer your gift. Come to terms quickly with your accuser while you are on the way to court with him, or your accuser may hand you over to the judge, and the judge to the guard, and you will be thrown into prison.

This, according to eschatologists, speaks of the need to forgive and be reconciled before a judgment is rendered and is best understood as part of the end-time putting of one's life in order.

What do we make of these notions? As I hope is evident by now, the second claim is highly dubious. Its basic premise is shaky at best, so any conclusion based on it must be judged as suspect if not an outright non sequitur. Furthermore, as we have seen with respect to a similar claim about the form of the verb in the "kingdom" petition, the third claim here rests on a misunderstanding of what the aorist imperative in this petition signifies.[45] But what about the remaining claims?

There is no doubt that part of Second Temple Judaism's view of the future involved a judgment on God's part of the wicked and the faithful. Jesus himself seems to have espoused that view, though it is highly questionable that he saw this event as a principal part of some end-of-time apocalyptic scenario rather than as a possible or probable historical event, as did the prophets before him when they spoke of God's impending judgment.[46] But the real problem here is that no reference to a future judgment, let alone a future forgiveness in the

---

45. See above, pp. 109.
46. Caird, *New Testament Theology*, 359-366; idem, *The Language and Imagery of the Bible* (Grand Rapids: Eerdmans, 1997), 255–60; See, too, N.T. Wright, *The New Testament and the People of God* (Minneapolis: Fortress Press, 1992), 280–89.

context of a divine judgment, appears or is in anyway alluded to in the forgiveness request. Moreover, Jesus nowhere else teaches that God's forgiveness of sinners will occur only in the future, let alone as a one-time event. It is, on the contrary, presently and constantly available (see Mark 2:5; Luke 7:48). So the idea that the horizon of the request is some great expected assize is dubious. The meaning and significance of the aorist tense of the imperative in the request is misconstrued if it is taken as evidence in this regard. Its use here has more to do with emphasizing how heartfelt the request is and indicating under what conditions one might expect the request to be met than it does in implying that the forgiveness spoken of is a once-only event. In Matt. 5:23-25, the issue at hand is "settling accounts" with an accuser, which is not a theme found in the request. So the interpretation of the request as an eschatological one is forced.

One should note, too, that behind the eschatological view of the request stands a questionable hidden assumption, namely, that when Jesus gives his disciples the forgiveness request, he views them as sinners who are in need of God's forgiveness. But nothing here or in the rest of the Disciples' Prayer indicates this. Nothing like this is presupposed with respect to those who are told to forgive anyone who sins against them in such notable Jewish parallels to the request as Sir. 27:30—28:7:

> Anger and wrath, these also are abominations, yet a sinner holds on to them. The vengeful will face the Lord's vengeance, for he keeps a strict account of all their sins. Forgive your neighbor the wrong he has done, and then your sins will be pardoned when you pray. Does anyone harbor anger against another, and expect healing from the Lord. If one has no mercy toward another like himself, can he then seek pardon for his own sins? If a mere mortal harbors wrath, who will make an atoning sacrifice for his sins? Remember the end of your life, and set enmity aside; remember corruption and death, and be true to the commandments. Remember the commandments, and do not be angry

with your neighbor; remember the covenant of the Most High, and overlook faults.

Or in sections of a work known as the *Testament of the Twelve Patriarchs*.

T. Zeb. 5: Have, therefore, compassion in your hearts, my children, because even as a man doeth to his neighbour, even so also will the Lord do to him.

T. Joseph. 18: If you [pl.] also, therefore, walk in the commandments of the Lord, my children, He will exalt you there, and will bless you with good things for ever and ever. And if any one seeks to do evil unto you, do evil unto you, do ye by well-doing pray for him, and ye shall be redeemed of the Lord from all evil.

Nor can it be found in teachings of Jesus that deal with the forgiveness of debts.

Like the "bread" request, then, the forgiveness request is not eschatological in intention. It is actually a declaration of intent—in this case, regarding the basis on which the disciples are willing to be judged as sinners.

And what is that basis? It is that they, like the God whose υἱοί they are, are willing to cancel or let go of (ἄφες [*aphes*] from ἀφίημι [*aphiēmi*] = "to cancel, remit, pardon") rightful claims to what is owed to them by "debtors" (τοῖς ὀφειλέταις ἡμῶν [*tois opheiletais hēmōn*]), that is, those who are legally and morally obligated to recompense them (the disciples) either for money borrowed and not repaid, for offenses to their person[47] and notably, as Bruce Chilton has shown, their enemies.[48]

---

47. ὀφειλέτης = "a debtor," i.e., one who is obligated to do something for someone, one who is guilty of a misdeed, including those who would bring down judgment from the Messiah and destruction from God upon one's head. On this, see Bruce A. Chilton, "Jesus and the Repentance of E. P. Sanders," *Tyndale Bulletin* 39 (1988): 10.

48. Chilton, "Jesus and the Repentance of E.P. Sanders," 10, who notes on the basis of the use in the Isaiah Targum of the Aramaic term *hwb'*, which most likely stands behind the word

THE DISCIPLES' PRAYER

To understand the significance of this we need to take into account two things: First, what it meant in the Mediterranean world of the first century to "forgive" debts that one was rightfully owed, and second, why the ruler in Matthew's parable of the unmerciful servant (Matt. 18:23-35) punishes this servant for not acting as generously toward one of his retainers as his master has acted toward him.

As Bruce Malina and others have shown, to cancel lawful debts, let alone to forgive one's enemies, without some good or mitigating reason was an action that brought intense shame on the one who did so. For in this, the one forgiving debt and offenses to his person (and his people) would be showing himself as a fool, as weak, as fearful of standing up for his rights, and as someone who, as we might say, was ready to let others "get away with murder."[49] Thus the promise of forgiveness to those who owe "debts" is the abandonment of the cultural criteria for maintaining one's honor when disgraced, through retaliation. It is a commitment to magnanimity, mercy, and peace, even if it means that others will see one remaining in disgrace.

Here is the parable of the unmerciful servant:

> Then Peter came to Jesus and asked, "Lord, how many times shall I forgive my brother when he sins against me? Up to seven times?" Jesus answered, "I tell you, not seven times, but seventy-seven times. "Therefore, the kingdom of heaven is like a king who wanted to settle accounts with his servants. As he began the settlement, a man who owed him ten thousand talents was brought to him. Since he was not able to pay, the master ordered that he and his wife and his children and all that he had be sold to repay the debt. "The servant fell on his knees before him. 'Be patient with me,' he begged, 'and I will pay back everything.' The servant's master took pity on him, canceled the debt

---

ὀφειλέτης, the "debtor" was a species of wicked Gentile (34.2) or an enemy of Jerusalem (54.17). See, too, J. B. van Zijl, *A Concordance to the Targum of Isaiah* (Missoula: Scholars Press, 1979), 5–58. Thus the meaning of "as we forgive those indebted to us" seems to be "as we forgive the enemies of Israel."

49. Bruce J. Malina, *The New Testament World: Insights from Cultural Anthropology*, 3rd ed. (Louisville: Westminster John Knox, 2001), 55.

and let him go. But when that servant went out, he found one of his fellow servants who owed him a hundred denarii. He grabbed him and began to choke him. 'Pay back what you owe me!' he demanded. His fellow servant fell to his knees and begged him, 'Be patient with me, and I will pay you back.' But he refused. Instead, he went off and had the man thrown into prison until he could pay the debt. When the other servants saw what had happened, they were greatly distressed and went and told their master everything that had happened. Then the master called the servant in. 'You wicked servant,' he said, 'I canceled all that debt of yours because you begged me to. Shouldn't you have had mercy on your fellow servant just as I had on you?' In anger his master turned him over to the jailers to be tortured, until he should pay back all he owed. This is how my heavenly Father will treat each of you unless you forgive your brother from your heart" (Matt. 18:23-35).

The parable begins with a king acting in a way quite uncharacteristic of any agrarian ruler. He forgives a debt of unimaginable proportions. But why? First, the king presides over subjects who are crippled by debt and who, therefore, in their inability to pay tribute and taxes frustrate his ability to rule. Second, the king needed his servant for the efficient administration of his kingdom. To throw the servant in jail would bung up the works, so to speak, since the servant was not easily replaceable. So, as J. Duncan M. Derrett has noted, "The release was for the good of the kingdom." It was but the first in a series of actions whose purpose was to "lighten the burdens of the provinces" and "oil all the wheels" for the well-being of the entire kingdom.[50] The great act of debt forgiveness was meant to initiate further acts of forgiveness of debt. The king has made it a point of honor, and he expects the servant to understand. He has broken the cycle of ruthless exploitation and extraction, and what the patron has done, the client must do. But the servant fails to imitate his master and instead engages in what William Herzog II has called the tactics

---

50. J. Duncan M. Derrett, *Law in the New Testament* (London: Darton, Longman & Todd, 1970), 42.

of a typical powerful bureaucrat. In doing so, he makes the king look like a fool, or worse, like a weak and gullible ruler without power over the behavior of his subjects. In other words, in not acting as his master has done, the servant disgraces his patron and brings his name into disrepute and thus backs the king into a corner.[51] Shades of not hallowing the ruler's name!

The upshot for our understanding of the forgiveness petition in the Disciples' Prayer, then, is that here again we find a concern not for praying down into the present age something that properly belongs to Israel's future, but for maintaining a discipleship that is faithful to, and in action consistent with, the both the nature and character of God who shows mercy to the good and wicked alike and the way he fulfills his purposes, which includes loving Israel's enemies.

The "Temptation" Request

There remains the "temptation" request. Is it in any way eschatological? Since the claim that it is not only is widely believed but is also one of the linchpins of the eschatologists' case, I shall devote a full chapter to analyzing it.

Addendum: A Word about the Meaning of "Our Father" in the Invocation

Much has been written about Jesus' use of "Father" as an address to God, especially on the matters of whether it was unique to Jesus (it wasn't);[52] whether it expresses a consciousness on Jesus' part of a special and exclusive childlike relationship with God (it didn't);[53] and

---

51. On this, see William Hertzog II, *Parables as Subversive Speech* (Louisville: Westminster John Knox, 1994), 146–47.
52. See Crump, *Knocking on Heaven's Door*, 98; Scot McKnight, *A New Vision for Israel: The Teachings of Jesus in National Context* (Grand Rapids: Eerdmans, 1999), 50–54.
53. See especially James A. Barr, "'Abbā Isn't 'Daddy,'" *Journal of Theological Studies* 39 (1988): 28–47.

whether it reveals something of Jesus' understanding of the nature and character of God (it does).⁵⁴ These are all interesting questions. But as far as unlocking the function that Jesus intended the address to have when it was uttered by his disciples, these, with the exception of the last point, are side issues.

As Mary Rose D'Angelo has shown, the primary function of the address "Father" is to affirm three things: that it is the God of Israel alone, and not another singular claimant to the title, who deserves to be called and acknowledged as "Father"; that the disciples are intent to pledge their filial loyalty to the God of Israel and to serve him as he decrees faithful υἱοί θεοῦ should; and that the God of Israel is recognized both as their refuge, when "sonship" becomes costly, and as the one who can prevent them from falling into apostasy.⁵⁵

The first point becomes clear when we recognize that Jews in first-century Palestine were beset with claims from their Roman conquerors that the emperor, who bore the titles *parens patriae* and *pater patriae*, not only was the true and only father of the peoples over whom he held sway, but also deserved to be acknowledged as such because he had brought peace and security to the world.

The second needs little comment or buttressing. One does not address another as "father" unless one is placing oneself under that person's authority and pledging to be governed by his will.

The proof of the third point lies in the fact that in such prayers as 4Q372 1:16-20; Joseph and Aseneth 12:8-15; 3 Macc. 6:3-4, 7-8; and Sir. 23:1, in which God is also addressed as "Father," this address is presented as particularly appropriate specifically for υἱοί of God who,

---

54. Crump, *Knocking on Heaven's Door*, 104–6; McKnight, *A New Vision for Israel*, 55–69; Joseph A. Fitzmyer, "*Abba* and Jesus' Relation to God," in *A cause de l'Évangile. Études sur les Synoptiques et les Actes offertes au P. Jacques Dupont, O.S.B.*, Lectio Divina 123 (Paris: Cerf, 1985), 16–38.
55. Mary Rose D'Angelo, "Abba and 'Father': Imperial Theology and the Jesus Traditions," *Journal of Biblical Literature* 111, no. 4 (1992): 611–30.

because of facing affliction and persecution from the wicked and the oppressor, fear that they might apostatize.

6

The "Temptation" Petition

As I have noted above, the request καὶ μὴ εἰσενέγκῃς ἡμᾶς εἰς πειρασμόν (*kai mē eisenenkēs hēmas eis peirasmon*) has been taken by the advocates of an eschatological interpretation as the disciples' plea to God that they might be prevented either (1) from ever experiencing the woes of the great "end-time" tribulation that Jews in Jesus' day expected to beset the people of God at the dawning of the long-awaited age of salvation, or (2) from showing themselves faithless should they be plunged into these woes. Does this view have any merit? Let's look at three assumptions undergirding it.[1]

---

1. The either/or here depends on whether one thinks the expression εἰσενέγκῃς . . . εἰς ("lead us . . . into") means (1) "to come up to (the boundary of something)"—so Stanley Porter, "Mt. 6:13 and Lk. 11:4: Lead us not into temptation," *Expository Times* 101 (1990): 360; Raymond E. Brown, "The Pater Noster as an Eschatological Prayer," in *New Testament Essays* (Garden City, NY: Doubleday, 1968), 315–17; B. Young, *Jewish Background to the Lord's Prayer* (Austin: Center for Judaic-Christian Studies, 1984) 31; Oscar Cullmann, *Prayer in the New Testament* (Minneapolis: Fortress Press, 1995), 58–60, 62–63; or (2) that it has the sense of "to penetrate into the interior (of something)"—so Joachim Jeremias *The Lord's Prayer* (Philadelphia: Fortress Press, 1964), 28–31; J. Carmignac, *Recherches sur le "Nôtre Père"* (Paris: Letouzay & Anè, 1969), 236–304, 437–45, following J. Heller, "Die Sechste Bitte des Vaterunser," *Zeitschrift für katholische Theologie* 25 (1901): 85–93, along with many other modern commentators and many

THE DISCIPLES' PRAYER

The first assumption is that whatever else first-century Jews did or did not believe about a coming age of salvation, a "great tribulation" involving unheard-of affliction for the people of God was thought to be a principal part of it.² The second is that the "temptation" spoken of in Matt. 6:13 // Luke 11:2 refers to this event. To quote Joachim Jeremias:

> This word (peirasmós in Greek) does not mean the little temptations or testings of every life, but the final great Testing which stands at the door and will extend over the whole earth—the disclosure of the mystery of evil, the revelation of the Antichrist, the abomination of desolation (when Satan stands in God's place), the final persecution and testing of God's saints by pseudo-prophets and false saviors. The final trial at the end is—apostasy! Who can escape?³

The third is that it is the disciples, and then by extension anyone else who "makes bold to say" the prayer of which the petition is a part, who are here thought of by Jesus as potentially engaged with or subjected to πειρασμός (peirasmos).⁴

---

ancient authorities including Dionysius of Alexandria (Patrologia Graeca 10:1601) and Hilary of Poitiers (*Tractatus in Psalmos* 115.111.15 [Patrologia Latina 9:510]).

2. The most recent full-scale defense of this claim is that of Brandt Pitre, *Jesus, the Tribulation, and the End of the Exile* (Grand Rapids: Baker Academic, 2006), 41–130.
3. Jeremias, *Lord's Prayer*, 29.
4. The names of commentators, both ancient and modern, who hold this position are far too many to list completely here. But among the earlier ones are Marcion (see Adolf von Harnack, *Marcion: The Gospel of the Alien God*, trans. John E. Steely and Lyle D. Bierma [Durham, NC: Labyrinth, 1990], 207), Tertullian (*De oratione* 8), Origen (*De oratione* 29.1–19; 30.1–3), Hilary (*Tractatus in Psalmos* 118, aleph, 15), Ps.-Ambrose (*De sacramentis* 5.4.29); Jerome (*Commentariorum in Ezechielem* 48.16) Cyprian (*De oratione Dominica* 25), Augustine (*De Serm. dom. in monte* 2.9.30), Luther (*Small Catechism*), Calvin (*Commentary on a Harmony of the Evangelists, Matthew, Mark, and Luke*, trans. William Pringle [Edinburgh: T&T Clark, 1895], 1:328–29). Among the numerous twentieth-century voices supporting this view are W. D. Davies and Dale C. Allison (*Matthew 1–7* [Edinburgh: T&T Clark, 1998], 1:613n51), Ulrich Luz (*Matthew 1–7*, Hermeneia [Minneapolis: Fortress Press, 2007], 384–88), Jeremias (*Lord's Prayer*, 28–31); C. F. D. Moule ("Unresolved Problem," *RThRev* 33 [1974]: 66–70, Ernst Lohmeyer (*The Lord's Prayer* [London: Collins, 1965], 191–208), Hans Dieter Betz (*The Sermon on the Mount: A Commentary on the Sermon on the Mount, Including the Sermon on the Plain (Matthew 5:3—7:27 and Luke 6:20–49)*, ed. Adela Yarbro Collins, Hermeneia [Minneapolis: Fortress Press, 1995], 405–13), G. B. Caird (*St. Luke* [London: Pelican, 1963], 152), I. Howard

But do these assumptions have any validity? My answer is no. Take the first one. As Richard Horsley has recently pointed out,

> The scholarly impression that a great tribulation would be a principal event in the supposed "apocalyptic scenario" [of first-century Judaism] may be the result of tricks that their own translation and literal reading [of Jewish apocalyptic texts] played on the scholars. There is no reference to a special time of tribulation or suffering in any of the second-temple apocalyptic texts, except for the brief statement in Daniel 12:2b ["And many of those who sleep in the dust of the earth shall awake, some to everlasting life, and some to shame and everlasting contempt"].[5]

Nor, he notes, may the "suffering" in Mark 13:19, 24a, be appealed to as a reference to first-century belief in an eschatological "time of trial." For this passage refers not to some special period of time in an end-of-the-world scenario, but to the effects of Roman military attacks on Jerusalem or acts of repression and persecution by Roman client rulers—that is, to historical and political, not "end-time," conflict and distress.[6] If there is any notion in these texts of an expectation of a future increase of suffering and woes for the people of Israel, it is there not because of a belief in an eschatological

---

Marshall (*The Gospel of Luke*, New International Greek Testament Commentary [Grand Rapids: Eerdmans, 1978], 461).

That orants of the petition have, from at least the third century onward, generally assumed that it is believers (including themselves individually) whom the petition envisages as the ones potentially engaged with or subjected to πειρασμός, is clear from (1) the various embolisms on the petition that were (and continue to be) offered by a celebrant when the Lord's prayer is recited in various liturgies and from (2) the glosses attached to the petition in both the Eastern and Western catechetical tradition.

For examples of early Byzantine, Syriac, Coptic, and Alexandrine embolisms, as well as instances of Greek and Latin glosses that show the universality of this view among orants of the Lord's Prayer, see G. G. Willis, "Lead Us Not into Temptation," *Downside Review* 93 (1975): 281–88.

5. Richard Horsley, *Prophet Jesus and the Renewal of Israel: Moving Beyond a Diversionary Debate* (Grand Rapids: Eerdmans, 2012), 45–46.

6. As to what may be gleaned on this matter from Rev. 3:10 ("Because you have kept my word of patient endurance, I will keep you from the hour of trial which is coming on the whole world, to try those who dwell upon the earth"), see below.

scenario, but because of what could be deduced as likely to occur given recent experience with these (and previous) rulers and their known intent to continue the repressions they had engaged in during the recent past. Indeed, the whole scholarly notion, rampant in New Testament studies since Johannes Weiss's "(re)discovery" of "apocalyptic," that Jews expected *any* kind of cosmic catastrophe, let alone the imminent end of the world, as part of the outworking of any divinely grounded hope for Israel, may be a false one, since it may be based in an overly literal reading, and misunderstanding of the nature, of "apocalyptic" texts.[7]

What of the second assumption? It fares no better. While it is true, as I've noted previously, that πειρασμός does, as the eschatologists claim, mean "a test of faithfulness," there is absolutely no evidence that it referred to the "final/eschatological test," the test of faithfulness to which believers were (supposedly) to be subjected at the "end of the age." Not one instance can be found among any of the many extant pre-150-CE occurrences of the noun that gives any hint whatsoever that πειρασμός was a recognized term for this climactic test.[8] True, Rev. 3:10, which has Jesus promising the Philadelphians

---

7. The literature challenging the "standard" and until recently almost universal view of Jewish apocalyptic eschatology is growing. A good place to begin is with the section on the language of apocalyptic in George Caird's *The Language and Imagery of the Bible* (Philadelphia: Westminster, 1980), 243–71.

8. Luz, *Matthew 1–7*, 384. The noun πειρασμός is found most frequently in literature in the Greek biblical tradition, where it appears with some frequency. It occurs thirteen times in the Septuagint (Exod. 17:17; Deut. 4:34; 6:16; 7:19; 9:22; 29:3[2]; Ps. 94[95]:8; Eccles. 3:10; 4:8; 5:2, 13; 8:16, if we accept as authentic the reading of Alexandrinus in Eccles. 3:10; 4:8; and 8:16 [B and Sinaiticus have περισπασμός], of Sinaiticus in 5:13 [A and B have περισπασμός], and of the three main textual witnesses in 5:2; on the Hebrew equivalents of πειρασμός in these instances, see below), seven times in the Apocrypha of the Septuagint (Sir. 2:1; 6:7; 27:5, 7; 36[33]:1; 44:20; 1 Macc. 2:52), twice in the Pseudepigrapha (Testament of Joseph 2:7; Fragment of Greek Jubilees W on Jub. 10.8 [text in *Pseudepigrapha Veteris Testamenti Graece*, ed. A. M. Denis and M. DeJonge, vol. 3, *Fragmenta Pseudepigraphorum Quae Supersunt Graeca*, ed. A. M. Denis (Leiden: Brill, 1970), 87]), once in the extant fragments of non-Septuagintal Greek versions of the Hebrew Scriptures (Symmachus, Gen. 44:15), and, not including Matt. 6:13 // Luke 11:4, nineteen times in the New Testament (Mark 14:38; Matt. 26:41; Luke 4:13; 8:13; 11:14; 22:40; 46; Acts 15:26 [D E]; 20:19; 1 Cor. 10:13 [twice]; Gal. 4:14; 1 Tim.

that "Because you have kept my word of patient endurance, I will keep you from the hour of trial that is coming on the whole world to test the inhabitants of the earth" might at first glance seem to be an exception to this. But two things need to be noted. In the first place, in Rev. 3:10, πειρασμός not only is arthrous (i.e., it is accompanied

---

6:9; Heb. 3:18; James 1:2, 12; 1 Pet. 1:16; 2 Pet. 2:9; Rev. 3:10). In the so-called Apostolic literature composed before 150 CE, πειρασμός appears at least four times—once in the Didache (8.2), once in Hermas (*Man.* 9.7), once in Polycarp's *Epistle to the Philippians* (7.2.5), once in a fragment of Ignatius's *To Polycarp* (fragment 25, from e cod. Florent. Laur. 6.4 [*Ad Polycarpum*] in J. H. Crehan, "A New Fragment of Ignatius' *Ad Polycarpum*," *Studia Patristica* 1 [Texte und Untersuchungen] 63 [1957]: 24)—and nine times if we accept a relatively early date for both the Acts of Paul, where the noun appears four times (Acts of Paul and Thecla 25.6; 25.9; 40.7; *Recenscion C Codex E* 5.14), and 2 Clement, where πειρασμός appears once (*2 Cor.* 39.7).

But πειρασμός also occurs in pre-150-CE "secular" literature at least ten times. Πειρασμός appears once in a section of the work by the (probably) second-century-BCE grammarian Ptolemaeus of Ascalon titled *De differentia vocabulorum* (Sigma 146, according to the enumeration of the work in the edition of *De differentia vocabulorum* edited by V. Palmieri in *Annali della Facolta di Lettere e Filosofia dell' Universita di Napoli* 24 [1981–1982]: 191–225), once in the preface to the *Materia Medica*, a work on the medicinal properties of plants and the effects of drugs by the first-century-CE physician and pharmacologist Pedanius Dioscorides (*De materia medica*, pref. 5.12), once in the *Partitiones*, a work by the first-century Alexandrian grammarian Aelius Herodianus (*Partitiones* 110.5, ed. J. F. Boissonade, *Herodiani paertitiones* [London, 1819]), three times in what I take to be a pre-second-century-CE commentary by an anonymous author on Aristotle's *Art of Rhetoric* (In *Anonymi in Aristotelis Artem Rhetoricum* 98.29 [on *Rhet.* 2.4 (1381b) 27]; 102.29 [on *Rhet.* 2.5 (1383a) 17]; 103.9 [on *Rhet.* 2.5 (1383a) 18]), once in an a pre-second-century anonymous commentary on Aristotle's *Nichomachean Ethics* (*Anonymi in Aristotelis Ethica: In Ethica Nichomachea Commentaria* 454.10 [on Nichomachean Ethics 7.13 (1153b) 17]), once in an early *Scholion* on Euripides's *Hecuba* (*Scholia in Eupripdes*, sch. *Hecuba* 1226, which appears in Cod. Vat. 909), once in the *Syntipas* (V. Jernstedt and P. Nikition, ed., *Memories de l'Academie Imperiale des Sciences de St. Petersbourg, 8me Serie, Classe des Sciences historico-philologique* 11, no. 1. [1912]: 124), an anonymous first-century-CE Arabian Nights, and once in the *Cyranides* (Βιβλοι Κυράνιδες or Κοιράνιδες) (see F. de Mely and C.-E Ruelle, *Les Lapidaries de l'antiquite et du moyen age*, vol. 2, *Le Lapidaries grecs* (1898), sec. 40.24), a first-century-CE work on magical curative powers of plants, stones, and animals.

If we were to cast our net even wider to include biblically related literature composed before the end of the second century CE, then our number of occurrences would increase by at least twenty additional instances. For πειρασμός is used twice in the Acts of John (at 21.13 in the main text and 16.6 in the recension), eight times in the writings of Clement of Alexandria (at *Protrepticus* 9.84.3; *Stromata* 1.9.44; 1.17.86; 4.6.41; 4.7.47 [a quotation from 1 Peter]; 4.20.129 [a quotation of 1 Peter]; 7.12.76; *Excerpta ex Theodoto* 4.84.1), and ten times in the later Pseudo-Clementines (*Epistle of Clement to James* 2.3; 14.3; *Hom. 2* 39.1; *Hom. 16* 13.2; 13.5; 21.4; *Hom. 18* 20.2; 20.4; *Epitome Prior* 145.10 [= *Epistle of Clement to James* 2.3]; *Epitome Altera* 146.6 [= *Epistle of Clement to James* 2.3]).

by the definite article), as πειρασμός in the "temptation" request is not, but, as Robert H. Gundry has pointed out, it also needs the help of the accompanying expressions "the hour" and "coming upon the world to test the ones dwelling upon the earth" in order to carry a reference to the great test expected to wind up the present age.[9] We should also note the implications of the fact, pointed out by Schuyler Brown, that those whom the seer says are to experience the particular πειρασμός spoken of in Rev. 3:10, namely, "the inhabitants of the earth" (τοὺς κατοικοῦντας ἐπὶ τῆς γῆς), are actually not Christians, but the persecutors of the church.[10] So here the evidence indicates that even should πειρασμός mean "the final test of apocalyptic expectation," it was thought of as something the enemies of believers, not believers themselves, would experience.[11] Therefore the use of the term in Rev. 3:10 is no evidence that anarthrous πειρασμός—that is to say, πειρασμός as it appears in the "temptation" request in the Disciples' Prayer—was, as advocates of the "final/eschatological test" opine, a recognized and recognizable technical term for the ultimate crisis of apocalyptic expectation.[12] On the contrary, as C. F. D. Moule has observed, "It only shows how carefully it [πειρασμός] is defined and given the article when it has to mean this [i.e., "eschatological test"]."[13] In other words, Rev. 3:10 is the exception that proves the rule.

Along these same lines, if Matthew and Luke had wanted it to be understood that Jesus had originally told his disciples to pray for protection against some "final testing," let alone "the final testing" of apocalyptic expectation, then they might have used something

---

9. Robert H. Gundry, *Mark: A Commentary on His Apology for the Cross* (Grand Rapids: Eerdmans, 1995), 872.
10. S. Brown, "The Hour of Trial (Rev. 3:10)," *Journal of Biblical Literature* 85 (1966): 309.
11. Note, too, that according to Rev. 3:10 it is only the Philadelphians, and not Christians in general, who are promised protection from the fallout of their enemies being "tried."
12. Luz, *Matthew 1–7*, 384. So also Carmingac, *Recherches*, 340–41.
13. Moule, "Unresolved Problem," 67.

like ἡ ἡμέρα θλιψέως (*hē hēmera thlipseōs*, "the day of tribulation") or καιρός θλιψέως (*kairos thlipseōs*, "time of tribulation") or simply θλιψίς (*thlipsis*, "tribulation"), instead of anarthrous πειρασμός.[14] The fact that neither Matthew nor Luke does so strongly indicates that for them the πειρασμός referred to in the "temptation" request of the Disciples' Prayer does not signify "the final/eschatological trial," even should there have been a conception of it in first-century Judaism.

Does the third assumption—that πειρασμός equals the testing of disciples' faithfulness—fare any better than the previous two did? To answer this, let's begin by taking note of the function that the petition takes on when we assume that it is the disciples who are envisioned in the petition as the object of πειρασμός, and then ask whether this function is plausible.

If the disciples were the subject of πειρασμός, then the petition would function to secure divine aid for the disciples, God's υἱοί, against their ever experiencing a present test of their own faithfulness or integrity. But how plausible is it that Jesus was urging the disciples in the "temptation" request to ask for protection against their ever

---

14. It might, of course, be countered that Luke at least does indeed do this, if only indirectly, and therefore provides a witness to what the noun in Matt. 6:13 // Luke 11:2 was intended to mean. After all, as Marshall (*Luke*, 326) and Seesemann ("πειρα, κτλ," *TDNT* 6 [1968]: 31) note, Luke's substitution of ἐν καιρῷ πειρασμοῦ (*en kariō peirasmou*) for Mark's (γενομένης) θλίψεως ([*henomenēs*] *thlipseōs*) in his redaction of Mark's parable of the sower (see Mark 4:17; cf. Luke 8:13) seems to indicate that Luke regards θλιψίς and πειρασμός as synonymous. But, even if so (see Schuyler Brown, *Apostasy and Perseverance in the Theology of Luke* [Rome: Pontifical Biblical Institute, 1969], 14–15, who argues that Luke did not regard θλιψίς and πειρασμός as synonymous terms; and Hans Conzelmann [*The Theology of St. Luke* (New York: Harper & Row, 1961), 90], who argues that at 8:13 Luke has substituted πειρασμός for Mark's θλιψίς in order to avoid a term with eschatological associations!), we should note that the θλιψίς/πειρασμός Luke speaks of at Luke 8:13 is not the "final test" and is not grounded in a/the crisis brought about by the apocalyptic woes of the "end times." Rather, since the θλιψίς Luke refers to is a θλίψεως ἢ διωγμοῦ διὰ τὸν λόγον (Mark 4:17)—that is, as Marshall also notes (*Luke*, 326), one that occurs as the believer tries during "ordinary times" to live a life of faithfulness—it is one arising from the persecution of believers envisaged as occurring well before the onset of the end of the age and therefore hardly "eschatological." So it is not likely, even if Luke viewed πειρασμός as a cipher for θλιψίς, that he viewed or intended the πειρασμός of Lk. 11:4b to be seen as the expected final θλιψίς.

experiencing such a test? If we take into account all that the biblical witness reveals about the nature of "testing" vis-à-vis the people of God, or *any* who would be among God's elect, the answer is: not at all.

In the first place, as is shown by even a cursory review of the context of the biblical and early Jewish instances of πειρασμός in which υἱοί/the elect and their faithfulness are said to be subjected to πειρασμός,[15] the "testing" of believers' faithfulness was known to be unavoidable.[16] Indeed, not only was πειρασμός perceived of as the inevitable consequence of being a "son of the covenant" (Sir. 2:1);[17] but it was even thought to be a desideratum. For to be subjected to a "testing of one's faithfulness" was viewed as a way both of reducing all doubt of how much an individual or a community loved God (Ps. 26:2 [LXX 25:2]; cf. Pss. 139:1, 23 [LXX 138:1, 23]) as well as of knowing that one was the object of God's fatherly love and concern (Wis. 3:1-6; 11:9; 12:20-22; 2 Macc. 6:12-16: Jdth. 8:25-27; Ps. Sol.

---

15. "Biblical" instances of πειρασμός used for a "testing of faithfulness or integrity" experienced by men include Gen. 44:15 (Symmachus); Deut. 4:34; 7:19; 29:2; Eccles. 3:10[A]; 4:8[A]; 5:2[A B S], 13[S]; 8:16[A]; Sir. 2:1; 6:7; 27:5, 7; 36(33):1; 44:20; 1 Macc. 2:52; Testament of Joseph 2:7; fr. G. Jubilees W (Jub. 10:8); Luke 4:13; 8:13; 22:28; Acts 15:26 DE; 20:19; 1 Cor. 10:13; Gal. 4:14; 1 Tim. 6:9; James 1:2, 12; 1 Pet. 1:6; 2 Pet. 2:9. See also Gen. 22:1; Exod. 15:25; 16:4; 20:20; Deut. 8:2, 16; 13:3; 33:8; Judg. 2:22; 3:1, 4; 2 Chron. 32:31; Ps. 25(26):2; 34(35):16; Dan. 12:10; Wis. 2:17, 24; 3:5; 11:9; Sir. 4:17; 13:11; 31(34):10; 37:27; Tob. 12:13; Jth. 8:25-26, where the cognates of πειρασμός, πειράζω, and ἐκπειράζω, as well as the noun's synonym, δοκιμασία, are so used.
16. This also is the import of the texts that use πειράζω and ἐκπειράζω to speak of the testing of God's elect. Moreover, it also stands behind the rabbinic notion, found at Numbers Rabbah 15:12; Canticles Rabbah II, 16:2, and elsewhere, that those whom God would elevate he first "tests."
17. See also Ps. 11:5; Prov. 3:12. See further Birger Gerhardsson, *The Testing of God's Son (Matt 4:1-11 and Par)* (Lund: Gleerup, 1966), 32-33.

13:9; 18:4).¹⁸ In other words, it was a cause not for fear, nor for any feeling of helplessness, but, as the James 1:2 remarks, for rejoicing.¹⁹

In the second place, if we accept as authentic the dominical agraphon quoted by Tertullian in his *De baptismo* 20.2, that "no one can obtain the kingdom of heaven who has not passed through testing,"²⁰ we have testimony that Jesus himself was known by the early church to have held and proclaimed these views.

In the face of these considerations, the idea that we have in the "temptation" request, urged by Jesus on the disciples, the hope that they be spared ever coming in contact with a πειρασμός of their own faithfulness proves difficult to accept. Not only does it make inexplicable why Jesus would call his disciples to utter such a plea, but it also presents us with what Moule calls an "unresolved problem":

> Why should anyone pray to escape testing—even if it is testing by the Devil and constitutes temptation [enticement to evil]? If one knows that testing and temptation are inevitable; if one knows that, before

---

18. On this, see Gerhardsson, *Testing of God's Son*, 32–33. In this regard, the text of Jdth. 8:25-27 is instructive: "In spite of everything let us give thanks to the Lord our God, who is putting us to the test as he did our forefathers. Remember what he did with Abraham, and how he tested Isaac, and what happened to Jacob in Mesopotamia in Syria, while he was keeping the sheep of Laban, his mother's brother. For he has not tried us with fire, as he did them, to search their hearts, nor has he taken revenge upon us; but the Lord scourges those who draw near to him, in order to admonish them."
19. Πᾶσαν χαρὰν ἡγήσασθε, ἀδελφοί μου, ὅταν πειρασμοῖς περιπέσητε ποικίλοις. Cf. James 1:12; 1 Pet. 1:6. Pertinent here is the judgment of Ceslas Spicq ("πεῖρα, κτλ," in *Theological Lexicon of the New Testament* [Peabody, MA: Hendrickson, 1994]), who sees that behind the New Testament usage of πειρασμός with men as the noun's object lies a conception of "testing of the faithfulness of a believer," which centers on the experience of hardships that may occur in varied forms and with greater or lesser intensity at any time in a believer's life but that is always thought to be providential, even when it appears in its most pronounced form, namely, "tribulation"—"painful and dangerous personal or social conditions that put the everyone's faithfulness to the test." It is: "a test of a Christian's authenticity [and] for the participants in Christ's suffering. . . . It is a purification, like that of metal in a furnace. This marvelous fruitfulness makes it possible to understand that for a believer under the new covenant the most dangerous and painful *peirasmos* can be a source and even gladness; [indeed] Jesus had commanded to bear fruit by persevering." (3:88).
20. "Neminem intemptatum regna caelestia consecuturum." For discussion and a defense of the authenticity of the saying, see Joachim Jeremias, *Unknown Sayings of Jesus* (London: SPCK, 1964), 73–74.

the glorious climax of God's final triumph, there will be inescapable testing of an exceptionally severe kind; if, moreover, one knows that testing can be salutary and that the Lord himself has pioneered the way through it to spiritual effectiveness—then what is the logic of praying for exemption?[21]

The answer to Moule's question is, of course, that there is none.[22]

To be sure, claims have been made to the contrary. C. F. W. Smith, for instance, has argued that while admittedly there would be a contradiction in praying καὶ μὴ εἰσενέγκῃς ἡμᾶς εἰς πειρασμόν when the πειρασμός in view had to do with something believers ordinarily experience, a prayer for escape or exemption from an anticipated "testing" nevertheless makes perfect sense if we adopt what he calls "the very profitable solution" of supposing that the πειρασμός of the petition refers "primarily to the final time of trial, the messianic woes."[23] Given the extraordinary nature of these times and the extreme threat to faithfulness they represent, a prayer for "escape" or exemption from being subjected to them is, Smith opines, something we should expect Jesus to urge on his disciples, something that they themselves would be eager to pray even without prompting.[24] Moule himself has put forward the view that in the end, although we may recognize that to pray for escape from πειρασμός

---

21. Moule, "Unresolved Problem," 71.
22. Noted, if only indirectly, by Julius Schniewind in his remarks that the petition confronts us with an insoluble contradiction of thought (*Das Evangelium nach Matthäus* [Gottingen: Vandenhoeck & Ruprecht, 1964], 88).
23. C. F. W. Smith, "The Lord's Prayer," IDB (Nashville: Abingdon Press, 1962) 3:157.
24. Ibid. Smith's "solution" is also that of Lohmeyer (*Lord's Prayer*, 203–9) and Brown ("Pater Noster," 316–17), Jeremias (*Lord's Prayer*, 29) and for the same reasons. Like Smith, Lohmeyer, Brown, and Jeremias recognize that since a believer's undergoing of πειρασμός is so often viewed in both the Old Testament and New Testament as salutary, and that consequently praying for escape from experiencing πειρασμός is not biblical, what the petition has to have in mind is a type of πειρασμός that, given its nature, was perceived to be more likely, if experienced, to result in the fall rather than the exaltation of the believer. The New Testament notion of "the final testing," they argue, admirably fills the bill, since, as such texts as Mark 13:19-20; 14:38; Rev. 3:10; and Matt. 6:13b purportedly show, it is then that all the forces of Satan will be unleashed in one final and almost irresistible onslaught against the elect of God. Who would not wish, they ask, to be spared this test?

is indeed not biblical and therefore involves a "*logical* inconsequence," the petition itself still makes psychological sense insofar as one might wish to avoid even what one recognizes is inevitable; indeed, not praying to escape πειρασμός is, in the light of human weakness, a form of hubris.[25]

But Smith's view rests on an assumption about the nature of the πειρασμός referred to in the "temptation" request that, as we have seen, has no real standing. In any case, even if πειρασμός did here signify "the final/eschatological test," this denotation would not really diminish the difficulty I have noted, since it is recognized in the biblical witness that even "eschatological trial" could be providential and salutary.[26] Moule's "solution" to the conundrum is, as Hans Dieter Betz has pointed out,[27] beset with two problems: (1) It resorts to the theological presupposition "that religious truth is in essence illogical, that is, irrational" and, however much it might stand as an impressive testimony to religious humility and contain insight into the paradoxes of human behavior, it nevertheless "confirms psychology not theology"; and (2) it runs roughshod over the fact that the words of the petition do not say what they are made by Moule to say. Indeed, as Moule himself admits, the trouble with his "solution" is that "all the rest of the traditions of Jesus' teaching emphasizes the inevitability of suffering, and do not bid the disciples [to] pray for escape."[28]

I conclude, then, given the biblical teaching on the inevitability of πειρασμός for those who would serve God, that it makes no sense for Jesus to urge the disciples to pray for exemption from experiencing or

---

25. Moule, "Unresolved Problem," 75 (emphasis original). Similarly, M. H. Sykes, "And Do Not Bring Us to the Test," ExpT 73 (1961–62): 189–90; Cullmann, *Prayer*, 62–66; J. Lowe, *The Lord's Prayer* (Oxford: Clarendon, 1962), 47, and many other commentators.
26. See Daniel 12. See also Eduard Schweizer, *The Good News according to Matthew* (Atlanta: John Knox, 1975), 156.
27. Betz, *Sermon on the Mount*, 410.
28. Moule, "Unresolved Problem," 75.

ever coming into contact with it.[29] Therefore we should rule out the possibility that the πειρασμός, the "testing of faithfulness," spoken of in the "temptation" request in the Disciples' Prayer, was meant by Jesus as a testing aimed at the disciples. On the contrary, I argue that the "temptation" spoken of here is, according to Jesus, one the disciples might aim at God. That is, in telling his disciples to pray "and do not lead us into temptation," Jesus was telling them to pray, "prevent us, God, from testing your faithfulness."

Before we go further on this point, we need to be clear about three things. First, what "putting God to the test" was thought to involve; second, how or when or why, according to the biblical witness, it was perpetrated; and third, how the activity was evaluated theologically.

---

29. Moule's observation that there really is no sense in praying for exemption from πειρασμός if the πειρασμός in the petition is taken as a "testing to be experienced by believers"—indeed, that taking πειρασμός to have this meaning, renders the petition illogical, if not absurd, and that it therefore cannot be what Matthew and Luke thought Jesus was saying when he urged his disciples to urge God μὴ εἰσενέγκῃς ἡμᾶς εἰς πειρασμόν—is supported by the peculiar way the petition is (mis)transmitted in the manuscript tradition or glossed by early commentators. For instance, Marcion reproduces it as "Do not suffer us to be led into 'testing'" (καὶ μὴ εἰσενέγκῃς ἡμᾶς εἰς πειρασμόν), a gloss that appears again in the early third century in a fragment of a work by Dionysius, bishop of Alexandria and pupil of Origen, who, when commenting on how the petition is to be understood, says, "that is, do not suffer us to fall into 'testing'" (καὶ δὴ καὶ μὴ εἰσενέγκῃς ἡμᾶς εἰς πειρασμόν· τουτέστι, μὴ ἐάσῃς ἡμᾶς ἐμπεσεῖν εἰς πειρασμόν [Patrologia Graeca 10:1601]). Tertullian rendered it "Do not allow us to be led into 'testing' by him who 'tests' (the devil)" ("Ne nos inducas in temptationem, id est, ne nos patiaris induci ab eo utique qui temptat," *De oratione* 8), and Cyprian recites it in the form "do not suffer us to be induced into 'testing'" ("et ne patiaris nos induci in temtationem"). In Codex Bobbiensis and the Itala we find "ne passus fueris induci nos in temptationem," and Chromatius of Aquila, Jerome, Augustine, and various Western liturgies gloss it as "Do not lead us into testing which we cannot bear" ("et ne nos inferas in temptationem quam suffere non possumus"/"ne inducas nos in temptationem quam ferre non possumus"). On all of this, see Willis, "Lead Us Not into Temptation," 281–88; A. J. B. Higgins, "Lead Us Not Into Temptation: Some Latin Variants," *Journal of Theological Studies* o.s. 46 (1945): 179–83.

The types of changes that appear in the tradition of variants, namely, (1) a qualification of the nature of the πειρασμός in view or (2) a transmutation of the plainly causative force of the petition into one that is permissive, testify to the immense difficulty that taking πειρασμός in Matt. 6:13 // Luke 11:2 to mean "a test of a believer's faithfulness" originally presented to anyone who was trying to make sense of the petition. Indeed, as Betz notes (*Sermon on the Mount*, 408–9), it is precisely a desire to remove or resolve this difficulty that stands as the motive force behind the attempts of both Jeremias and Carmignac, noted above, to show that καὶ μὴ εἰσενέγκῃς ἡμᾶς εἰς πειρασμόν has a permissive sense and is to be taken as originally meaning "cause us not to succumb to πειρασμός."

Here I can do no better than to quote the discussion of these matters found in *The Testing of God's Son* by Birger Gerhardsson. Beginning with the observation that the concept of "the testing of God" presupposes that God has established a covenant relationship with his "son," his elect, in which he has promised to protect and redeem those who are his, Gerhardsson remarks:

> To test God is to examine him to see if he will keep his obligations, challenging him to demonstrate his fidelity to the conditions of the covenant. It is usually a query raised by the covenant son, a demand that God should show by a powerful work, by a "proof" . . . or "sign" . . . that he really is the God of his people, is in their midst, is active as their saviour, protector and provider in accordance with his covenant promises. The action is condemned in the Old Testament as a very serious offense against God. What the sin consists of can scarcely be defined in one simple formula, but broadly speaking it is a violation of JHWH's divine honour for man to dictate to him; man is demonstrating his suspicion and *unbelief* in not regarding JHWH as trustworthy, reliable, faithful to the covenant (. . . πιστίς). To test God is thus the opposite of believing in him and therefore a very definite violation of the covenant bond. According to the Old Testament JHWH reacts in anger to exterminate his people.[30]

With this in mind, I think three things indicate that Jesus intended the πειρασμός referred to in the "temptation" request to be "the testing of God." First of all, the "testing of God" is not only a possible set meaning for the noun[31] but also the one that seems to be demanded by the logic of the petition. As we have seen in our analysis of the meaning of the expression καὶ μὴ εἰσενέγκῃς ἡμᾶς εἰς πειρασμόν, the experience or phenomenon here denoted by πειρασμός is perceived as something with which a "son" must have

---

30. Gerhardsson, *Testing of God's Son*, 28. For a similar evaluation of the concept of "testing God," see Seesemann, "πεῖρα, κτλ.," 27–28. The concept is fully explored by Korn, *ΠΕΙΡΑΣΜΟΣ, Die Versuchung des Glaubigen in der greischischen Bible* (Stuttgart: W. Kohlhammer, 1937), 32–43.
31. On this, see Gerhardsson, *Testing of God's Son*, 28–33; Seesemann, "πεῖρα, κτλ.," 32; BDAG, πειρασμός, 793.

THE DISCIPLES' PRAYER

no contact and should avoid at all costs. What meaning of πειρασμός fits better with this, given its connotations, than "the testing of God"?

Second, the request that contains our term πειρασμός is part of a prayer that, as we saw in chapter 3, begins with an exhortation on Jesus' part to his disciples to stand as "sons" of God who, instead of shaming God's name, will serve it and be in concert with God's will being done on earth (and therefore avoid all that resists its establishment: see Matt. 6:11-12 // Luke 11:2). In its language and intent, this prayer evokes themes at the core of the biblical "Massah" tradition, that is, the tradition about the wilderness generation's "putting God to the test" that is first spelled out in Exod. 17:1-7, Numbers 14, and Deuteronomy 6–8, and then reflected on elsewhere in both the Old and New Testaments and in rabbinic literature (see Pss. 78; 95; 106: Wis. 1:1-3; and 1 Corinthians 10 and the Epistle to the Hebrews).[32] It also echoes the substance of exhortations both (1) of Moses, found in Deut. 6:10-19, for Israel to hallow God's name, to obey him, and to see that his will is done,[33] and (2) of the author of the

---

32. On this, see H. Houk, "ΠΕΙΡΑΣΜΟΣ, the Lord's Prayer, and the Massah Tradition, [Ex 17:1-7]," *SJT* 19 (1966): 222-23. See also R. F. Cyster, "The Lord's Prayer and the Exodus Tradition," *Theology* 64 (1961): 377-81. Houk draws attention to the parallels between (1) the petition in Matt. 6:9//Lk. 11:2 that God's name be hallowed (ἁγιασθήτω τὸ ὄνομά σου and Exodus 19, with its notice of the restriction on the people not to go up the mountain with Moses as he journeys to receive the law; (2) the petition that God's kingdom come (ἐλθέτω ἡ βασιλεία σου) and the divine declaration at Exod. 19:5-6 that Israel "shall be my own possession among all peoples . . . and you shall be to me a kingdom of priests and a holy nation"; (3) the "bread" petition and the account in Exod. 16:4-5 of the giving of manna in the wilderness; and (4) the petition in Matt. 6:12 // Luke 11:4a that God forgive the petition's orants their sins (καὶ ἄφες ἡμῖν τὰς ἁμαρτίας ἡμῶν) and the exodus incident of Moses pleading with God to forgive the sins Israel committed in creating and worshiping the golden calf (Exod. 32:30-35).

33. The text reads: "And when the Lord your God brings you into the land which he swore to your fathers, to Abraham, to Isaac, and to Jacob, to give you, with great and goodly cities, which you did not build, and houses full of all good things, which you did not fill, and cisterns hewn out, which you did not hew, and vineyards and olive trees, which you did not plant, and when you eat and are full, then take heed lest you forget the Lord, who brought you out of the land of Egypt, out of the house of bondage. You shall fear the Lord your God; you shall serve him, and swear by his name [καὶ πρὸς αὐτὸν κολληθήσῃ καὶ τῷ ὀνόματι αὐτοῦ ὀμῇ]. You shall not go after other gods, of the gods of the peoples who are round about you; for the Lord your God in the midst of you is a jealous God; lest the anger of the Lord your God be kindled

book of Wisdom, who at Wis. 1:1-3 urges those in Israel who would "fear the Lord" to "love righteousness [and] think of the Lord with uprightness, and seek him with sincerity of heart." Now, we should note that in Deut. 6:10-19 and in Wis. 1:1-3 (and in the Massah tradition) this exhortation to hallow God's name and to see that God's will is done is explicated specifically in terms of an obligation on the part of those who consent to revere God's name to do so by avoiding putting him to the test. For Moses reminds the Israelites, "You shall not put the Lord your God to the test, as you tested him at Massah."[34] And the author of the book of Wisdom declares that "[God] is found by those who do not put him to the test, and manifests himself to those who do not distrust him,"[35] and that

> For perverse thoughts separate people from God,
> and when his power is tested [δοκιμαζομένη], it exposes the foolish.[36]

So with all of this echoed and evoked in the prayer of which our "temptation" petition is a part, the πειρασμός referred to is surely the activity of "testing God."

Third, there is the observation that seeing πειρασμός as bearing the meaning "the testing of God," and therefore referring to an activity that "sons" might engage in against him, creates no tension or contradiction (as the alternative "the testing of believers" most certainly does) with the meaning and intent of the petition that God

---

against you, and he destroy you from off the face of the earth. . . . You shall diligently keep the commandments of the Lord your God, and his testimonies, and his statutes, which he has commanded you. And you shall do what is right and good in the sight of the Lord, that it may go well with you."

34. Οὐκ ἐκπειράσεις κύριον τὸν θεόν σου, ὃν τρόπον ἐξεπειράσασθε ἐν τῷ Πειρασμῷ.
35. εὑρίσκεται τοῖς μὴ πειράζουσιν αὐτόν, ἐμφανίζεται δὲ τοῖς μὴ ἀπιστοῦσιν αὐτῷ.
36. On δοκιμάζω as a synonym for πειράζω, see R.C. Trench, "δοκιμάζω, πειράζω," in *Synonyms of the New Testament* (Grand Rapids: Eerdmans, 1948), 278. See too "δοκιμάζω," in *Greek-English Lexicon of the New Testament and Other Early Christian Literature*, ed. Frederick W. Danker, Walter Bauer, William F. Arndt, and F. Wilbur Gingrich, 3rd ed. (Chicago: University of Chicago Press, 2000), 255.

καὶ μὴ εἰσενέγκῃς ἡμᾶς εἰς πειρασμόν. Indeed, it resolves what is on the other view an unresolvable problem.

It follows that if πειρασμός here means "the testing of God," then given all that the idea of "the testing of God" connotes, the request in which the term appears must mean something like "prevent us, Father, from putting you to the test by doubting your ways and renouncing all that you have deemed fit for us to follow."

There are four reasons for regarding this as a correct interpretation of the text. The first is the often overlooked consideration that in the biblical tradition, seeking God's help to avoid engaging in πειρασμός against him is both a perfectly acceptable thing to pray for and something that God would be willing to grant.[37]

Second, although I have argued at length above against an eschatological interpretation of the Disciples' Prayer (in the sense of "praying down" into the present the yet-unrealized benefits of a future kingdom of God), the interpretation of the "temptation" petition that I am advancing here is consistent with understanding the Disciples' Prayer as a response to the actual dawning of the βασιλεία τοῦ θεοῦ in the ministry of Jesus (and might be considered "eschatological" in this limited sense). The prayer is formed in the light of the crises and καιρός for humanity that this situation brings about.[38] As apocalyptic literature, with all of its warnings about the

---

37. This certainly is the import of Heb. 3:7—4:1: "Therefore, as the Holy Spirit says, 'Today, when you hear his voice, do not harden your hearts as in the rebellion, on the day of testing in the wilderness, where your fathers put me to the test and saw my works for forty years. Therefore I was provoked with that generation, and said, 'They always go astray in their hearts; they have not known my ways.' As I swore in my wrath, 'They shall never enter my rest.' Take care, brethren, lest there be in any of you an evil, unbelieving heart, leading you to fall away from the living God. But exhort one another every day, as long as it is called 'today,' that none of you may be hardened by the deceitfulness of sin. For we share in Christ, if only we hold our first confidence firm to the end, while it is said, 'Today, when you hear his voice, do not harden your hearts as in the rebellion.' . . . Therefore, while the promise of entering his rest remains, let us fear lest any of you be judged to have failed to reach it."

38. As is argued by Jeremias, *The Lord's Prayer*, 26; Brown, "Pater Noster," 283; Lohmeyer, *Lord's Prayer*, 11; and many others.

dangers of apostasy, makes clear, it is after all in a time of crisis that υἱοὶ θεοῦ are most likely to engage in activity that is the essence of subjecting God to πειρασμός, namely, questioning, and then going on to reject the propriety or reasonableness or effectiveness of the way that God has constrained his elect to follow in faithfulness to him. What, then, would be more appropriate in such a situation than a prayer to have help in not putting God to the test? Indeed, it seems no small coincidence that we find the author of the Epistle to the Hebrews urging (albeit implicitly) just such a prayer on his readers when, as a result of their experiencing a crisis, they began to lose their confidence in the ways God had given them to live out their Christian confession (see Heb. 3:7-9).

The third consideration is that a call from Jesus for his disciples to pray for protection from "putting God to the test" is exactly what we should expect from Jesus, who knew that at the center of his own trials as Son to maintain his faithfulness to God was an inclination to put God to the test (cf. Matt. 4:7//Lk. 4:12). It is what we should expect if he was trying to shape his disciples to denounce, as he did, the wickedness and faithlessness of "this generation"; what we should expect if he wished them, as he himself did, to avoid showing themselves as in any way inclined to refuse to trust in God's providential care for them, or to express doubt that God's particular ways for them as his υἱοὶ were sufficient for achieving God's ends. As we have already seen, this is the biblical understanding of "putting God to the test."[39] In fact, it would be surprising if we did *not* find Jesus issuing so biblical a call for the disciples to petition God for help in avoiding putting God to the test.

---

39. A Son's refusal to trust in God's providential care and loving surveillance is expressly denoted as involving the Son in "testing God," a theme found not only in the Deuteronomic strand of the biblical witness but in the Wisdom tradition as well. See, e.g., Wis. 1:1–3:10; Sir. 18:23. For more on this, see Seesemann, "πεῖρα, κτλ.," 27–28; Gerhardsson, *Testing of God's Son*, 28–30.

The fourth consideration is that a call to the disciples to pray for protection from "putting God to the test" is not only something that Jesus would be likely to make. It is something that he does make, most significantly, in this same prayer, in his words to them about bread. As we have seen, that petition contains a reference to the "bread from heaven" referred to in Exod. 16:4,[40] the constraints on the receiving of which were the occasion for the faithless wilderness generation's grumbling (thus challenging God's good intentions toward his elect).[41] For the disciples to pray as υἱοὶ θεοῦ, "Father, *do* give us (now that it is) today our ἐπιούσιον bread,"[42] would in effect be to distinguish themselves from, and guard themselves against becoming, that community of υἱοὶ who had this same bread and yet, craving other food, spurned it as "worthless" (Numbers 11; Psalm 78) and demanded to be released from its constraint, thereby "testing God in their hearts" (as Psalm 78 notes; cf. Exod. 17:1-7; Num. 14:22; Ps. 95:6).[43]

The fifth consideration in favor of viewing the "temptation" request as asking for divine help to avoid πειρασμός against God is the implication of the fact that in the Markan parallel, Mark 14:38—a

---

40. See above, p. 148 n. 32.
41. See Numbers 11; 21; Deuteronomy 6; Psalms 78; 95. See also Gerhardsson, *Testing of God's Son*, 45–48.
42. My translation of the "bread" request reflects a view that the word σήμερον is to be taken as a reference not to when the ἐπιούσιον bread is to be given, but to a period of crisis (cf. Psalm 95) that has already begun, the very nature of which makes the acceptance of, and satisfaction with, the ἐπιούσιον bread all the more pointed. It is, I think, no coincidence that elsewhere in the New Testament, at Heb. 3:17-15; 4:7, when an injunction not to act as the wilderness generation is enjoined on believers, it is done under the consciousness of the arrival of God's "today."
43. It is worth noting again that of all the interpretations that have been made of the import of the "bread" request (on this, see W. Foerster, "ἐπιούσιος," in *TDNT*, ed. Gerhard Kittel and Gerhard Friedrich, trans. Geoffrey W. Bromiley, 10 vols. [Grand Rapids: Eerdmans, 1964–1976], 2:595-99), the one advocated here seems to be the only one that (1) not only creates no clash with dominical injunctions against anxiety over the cares of "the morrow" (see, e.g., Matt 6:34, μὴ οὖν μεριμνήσητε εἰς τὴν αὔριον, ἡ γὰρ αὔριον μεριμνήσει αὑτῆς· ἀρκετὸν τῇ ἡμέρᾳ ἡ κακία αὐτῆ, and Luke 12:21-31), (2) but also is fully consonant with the these injunctions' theological thrust.

text in which Jesus is presented, as he is Matthew and Luke, as urging his disciples to pray to be kept from "entering into" πειρασμός[44]—this is the stated objective.

Two observations make this clear. First, the often overlooked fact that in biblical usage, when the construction μή a form of ἔρχεσθαι εἰς is used in a command, as it is in Mark 14:38, with an object other than a place, the resultant phrase does not mean "do not encounter or succumb to [something]" but "do not commit or engage in [something],"[45] Consider, for instance, Ps. 142:2 (LXX), where, as K. Grayston notes, καὶ μὴ εἰσέλθῃς εἰς κρίσιν μετὰ τοῦ δούλου σου means, "do not engage in judging your servant."[46] Similarly, in Jer. 16:5 (LXX), the divine command Μὴ εἰσέλθῃς εἰς θίασον αὐτῶν obviously means "do not engage in mourning." And in Josh. 23:7, Joshua's final exhortation to the Israelites, μὴ εἰσέλθητε εἰς τὰ ἔθνη τὰ καταλελειμμένα ταῦτα, καὶ τὰ ὀνόματα τῶν θεῶν αὐτῶν οὐκ ὀνομασθήσεται ἐν ὑμῖν means "do not engage in the idolatrous practices which typify the nations."[47] Also note the positive form of the construction in Dan. 3:2—a royal command of Nebuchadnezzar to all his retainers and officers to "enter into" (ἐλθεῖν εἰς) the ἐγκαινισμός, the dedication ceremony, of a golden image he himself had "set up." Here the construction means "join in," "participate in"

---

44. (γρηγορεῖτε καὶ) προσεύχεσθε, ἵνα μὴ ἔλθητε εἰς πειρασμόν. On Mark's προσεύχεσθε, ἵνα μὴ ἔλθητε εἰς πειρασμόν as the imperatival form of the invocation [καὶ] μὴ εἰσενέγκῃς ἡμᾶς εἰς πειρασμόν, see Seesemann ("πεῖρα, κτλ.," 32) and Houk ("ΠΕΙΡΑΣΜΟΣ, the Lord's Prayer, and the Massah Tradition," 221–22). Indeed, as Raymond E. Brown (*The Death of the Messiah*, Anchor Bible Reference Library [New York: Doubleday, 1994], 1:197), following H. G. Meecham ("The Imperatival Use of ἵνα in the New Testament," *Journal of Theological Studies* 43 [1942]: 179–80), notes, ἵνα in Mark 14:38 is epexegetical, that is to say, it signifies that the phrase μὴ ἔλθητε εἰς πειρασμόν is the content of what Jesus commands his disciples to pray. Thus Mark 14:38 is both a parallel and an allusion to the tradition contained in the "temptation" request in the Disciples' Prayer.
45. Contra J. Carmignac, "'Fais que nous n'entrions pas dans la tentation,'" *Revue biblique* 72 (1965): 218–26.
46. K. Grayston, "The Decline of Temptation—and The Lord's Prayer," *SJT* 46 (1963): 292.
47. See also 1 Sam. 25:26 and 25:33, where μὴ ἐλθεῖν εἰς αἵματα (ἀθῷον) means "not committing murder."

the dedication ceremony. In the light of these observations, Jesus' words προσεύχεσθε, ἵνα μὴ ἔλθητε εἰς πειρασμόν must surely mean "pray that you might be kept from subjecting [someone or something] to a test of faithfulness." Given their syntax and its import, they are a command to Peter, James, and John to petition God for help against becoming agents, rather than victims, of such a test.

Second, consider what, according to Mark, prompts Jesus to command Peter, James, and John to pray ἵνα μὴ ἔλθητε εἰς πειρασμόν. As Mark 14:37 shows, Jesus' exhortation is prompted by the disciples' refusal to be willing to "stay awake" and to "watch" as the hour finally arrives in which Jesus allows himself, in obedience to the divine will, to be "delivered up to suffer many things" and to die on the cross—a refusal that culminates in the disciples abandoning Jesus and his ways, apparently rejecting as "of God" his call to them to follow him (see Mark 14:50; Matt. 26:56). Now, as Mark indicates elsewhere,[48] being willing to "stay awake" and "watch" is, among other things, to refuse to succumb to any doubt that God will provide, especially when it seems otherwise.[49] To "fall asleep" and to be unwilling to "watch" is equivalent to denying that God is faithful and that his ways are adequate to his purposes.[50] And, as we have seen (and as such texts as Exod. 17:1-7; Num. 14:22; Deuteronomy 6-8; Pss. 78; 95 [LXX]; Isa. 7:12; Wis. 1:1-3; Assumption of Moses 9:4; Matt. 4:1-11 // Luke 4:1-13; 1 Corinthians 10; Heb. 3:15-17; and, most notably, Mark 8:27-31 illustrate), denying that God is faithful and that his ways are adequate to what he claims are his purposes

---

48. See especially Mark 13:33-37. See also Matt. 24:42; 25:13; Mark 13:34-37; Luke 21:36; 1 Pet. 5:8.
49. On this, see T. J. Geddert, *Watchwords: Mark 13 in Markan Eschatology* (Sheffield: JSOT Press, 1989). W. L. Lane, *The Gospel According to Mark* (Grand Rapids: Eerdmans, 1974), 520.
50. Lane, *Mark*, 520; K. G. Kuhn, "New Light on Temptation, Sin, and Flesh in the New Testament," in *The Scrolls and the New Testament*, ed. Krister Stendahl (New York: Charles Scribner & Sons, 195), 94–113.

is the very essence of testing the faithfulness of God.⁵¹ Accordingly, what Mark presents as the occasion for Jesus to utter this command to Peter, James, and John that they should pray to be protected against becoming the agents of πειρασμός is his realization that they are on the verge of putting God to the test. In Mark's presentation, then, the "testing" against which Jesus commands Peter, James, and John to pray can be nothing other than the testing of God and his faithfulness. The objective of the petition in Mark 14:38 is help in refraining from putting God to the test. I argue that this is also the objective of the parallel request in the Disciples' Prayer.⁵²

Finally, the "temptation" request in the Disciples' Prayer is set out as coordinate with ἀλλὰ ῥῦσαι ἡμᾶς ἀπὸ τοῦ πονηροῦ (Matt. 6:13b).⁵³ This is itself a request for the community to be protected against putting God to the test. This is so especially (but not necessarily: see below) if, as the Eastern church and the Greek fathers have always held,⁵⁴ and as most modern commentators have claimed,⁵⁵ τοῦ πονηροῦ here is masculine, not neuter, and means "the

---

51. On this as the defining characteristic of "testing God," see above. See also Korn, *ΠΕΙΡΑΣΜΟΣ*, 32–43; Seesemann, "πεῖρα, κτλ," 27–28.
52. Notably, this conclusion follows especially if Mark 14:38 is a tradition that is dependent on or is derived directly from The Disciples' Prayer. In the first place, why would Mark give the petition the sense that it has for him if he did not see it as originally meaning "pray not to test God"? In the second place, neither Matthew nor Luke, who each reproduce Mark's scene of Jesus urging his disciples to pray "not to enter πειρασμός" (Matt. 26:41; Luke 22:40; cf. Luke 22:46), disagree with Mark in presenting the object of this prayer as help in refraining from putting God to the test. (Note that in both Matthew and Luke, the occasion for Jesus urging his disciples to "pray not to enter πειρασμός is the disciples' refusal to be willing to "stay awake" and to "watch" and Jesus' anticipation that they will abandon him, and thus reject as "of God" how he has called them to follow him.) Should we not have expected them to have done so if they understood the petition that Mark 14:38 mirrors to have had a meaning other than that which it has in the Markan account?
53. Also in the text of Luke 11:4 according to Sinaiticus1, A, C, D, R, and other witnesses.
54. On this, see especially J. B. Lightfoot, appendix 2, "The Last Petition of the Lord's Prayer" in *On a Fresh Revision of the English New Testament*, 3rd ed. (London: Macmillan, 1891), 307–9.
55. See, e.g., Carmignac (*Recherches*, 315), T. W. Manson, "The Lord's Prayer," *BJRL* 38 (1955–56): 446–48). Lohmeyer (*Lord's Prayer*, 210–17), Jeremias (*Lord's Prayer*, 29), Sykes ("And Do Not Bring Us to the Test," 190), Davies and Allison (*Matthew 1–7* 614–15), F. W. Chase (*The Lord's Prayer in the Early Church*, Texts and Studies: Contributions to Biblical and Patristic

evil one"—that is, "the devil."[56] Such texts as the Babylonian talmudic tractate Sanhedrin 89b (which I take to contain tradition dating from the first century CE); Apocalypse of Abraham 13 (see esp. vv. 9–13); the Testament of Job (especially in chs. 24–27); Mark 8:27-33; Luke 4:1-12; John 8:44; 2 Cor. 11:14; and especially Matt. 4:1-11 and Luke 4:1-13 show that the devil was regarded in Jesus' time as a being engaged principally in trying to get the pious to break or abjure a prior commitment to covenantal faithfulness to God by bringing them to express, and act on, the doubt that what God has commanded them to do (or put their trust in) is really "of God."[57] Whatever other functions this being may have been thought to have, he was ultimately and primarily thought of as the one who attempted to involve believers in "testing God" as Israel had tested him at Massah.[58]

Literature 1.3 [Cambridge: Cambridge University Press, 1891], 71–146), Joseph Blenkinsopp ("Apropos of the Lord's Prayer," *Heythrop Journal* 3 [1962]: 57n1), J. B. Bauer ("Libera nos a malo," *Verbum Domini* 34 [1956]: 12–15), Schweizer (*Good News according to Matthew* [Atlanta: John Knox, 1975] 156–57).

56. That the petition is *still* a request for the community to be protected against putting God to the test even if, as Augustine, many Western fathers after him, and others since have argued, is neuter and means "evil," see below. On the interpretation of the phrase by the Latin fathers, both before and after Augustine, see Lightfoot, "The Last Petition of the Lord's Prayer," 315–19. Modern advocates of τοῦ πονηροῦ as neuter include Schniewind (*Matthäus*, 88–89), H. Schurmann (*Das Gebet des Herrn* [Freiburg: Herder, 1958], 99–102), D. Hill (*The Gospel of Matthew* [London: Oliphants, 1972], 139), and G. Harder ("πονηρός, πονηρία," *TDNT* 6:560–61), who offers a full discussion of arguments for and against both readings of the phrase.

57. On this, see my *Temptations of Jesus in Early Christianity* (Sheffield: Sheffield Academic, 1995), 113–15. A brief review of the Babylonian talmudic tractate Sanhedrin 89b (full text in ibid., 113n86) bears out this claim nicely. Here Abraham, on the way to Mount Moriah to sacrifice Isaac as God has commanded him, is confronted by the devil, who has come to Abraham to carry out the divinely ordained "testing" of his (Abraham's) faithfulness. Notably, the devil does so specifically by trying to show Abraham, specifically through appeal to Scripture (Job 4:2-5; Job 4:6 and Job 4:12 combined with 4:7) and to the "knowledge" of God's ways he possesses by virtue of his privileged position as a member of the heavenly court (see the devil's remark "thus have I heard from behind the curtain"), that Abraham need not carry out God's command, for it is contrary to God's ways and not really what God demands of him.

58. This is clearly and indisputably stated in the Matthean and Lukan versions of the Synoptic stories of Jesus' "temptation" in the wilderness (Matt. 4:1-11 // Luke 4:1-13). Note how Jesus expressly declares that should he accede to the what the devil asks him to do as God's Son, he would then be guilty of a refusal to heed the particular commandment Moses gave to Israel to trust in God and οὐκ ἐκπειράσεις κύριον τὸν θεόν σου, ὃν τρόπον ἐξεπειράσασθε ἐν τῷ Πειρασμῷ (Deut. 6:16; see Matt. 4:7 // Luke 4:12). See also the story told with slight variations

Asking to be "delivered from the evil one," then, would be asking to be protected against solicitations and inclinations to subject God to πειρασμός. The petition ἀλλὰ ῥῦσαι ἡμᾶς ἀπὸ τοῦ πονηροῦ would also be a request for the community to be protected against putting God to the test if τοῦ πονηροῦ were taken as a neuter noun phrase. Then the phrase would mean "deliver us from *desiring or doing* evil." Why? In the first place, when τὸ πονηρόν is used as we find it here, that is, absolutely and not predicatively, it frequently denotes "*the* evil deed against God," "*the* bad one might plan or do against someone," "*the* wicked act humans do to someone."[59] In the second place, attached as it is to the petition καὶ μὴ εἰσενέγκῃς ἡμᾶς εἰς πειρασμόν, the interpretative context of the coordinate phrase ῥῦσαι ἡμᾶς ἀπὸ τοῦ πονηροῦ is the Massah tradition in Exod. 17:1-7; Numbers 14; Deuteronomy 6–8; and Psalms 78; 95; and 106, as well as the exhortation of Moses to Israel in Deut. 6:10-19. In this tradition, and presupposed in the Mosaic exhortation, the term τὸ πονηρόν signifies "desiring to do/or doing evil."[60] In the third place, there is the evidence of 1 Cor. 10:6 (Ταῦτα δὲ τύποι ἡμῶν ἐγενήθησαν, εἰς τὸ μὴ εἶναι ἡμᾶς ἐπιθυμητὰς κακῶν, καθὼς κἀκεῖνοι ἐπεθύμησαν). Here we find Paul engaged in the same sort of activity with which Jesus is engaged in Matt. 6:13b, namely, urging on believers the necessity of their praying to be delivered not from experiencing "evil" but from doing it.[61] As to what constitutes "desiring and/or doing evil," I think there is little doubt that it

---

by both Matthew and Mark, Matthew's of Jesus' confrontation with a satanic "testing" at Caesarea Philippi (Mark 8:27-33 // Matt. 16:13-23), where Jesus, in his rebuke to Peter (Mark 8:33 // Matt. 16:23), also declares that getting God's faithful to engage in putting God and his ways to the test is what stands behind much of Satan's activity.

59. See Lightfoot, "The Last Petition of the Lord's Prayer," 276; Harder, "πονηρός, πονηρία," 548–49, 552, 561–62.
60. See Deut. 4:25; cf. Deut 9:18; Harder, "πονηρός, πονηρία," 551.
61. That the term for "evil" here is κακόν is insignificant since κακόν is a synonym of τὸ πονηρόν. See W. Grundmann, "κακός, κτλ.," *TDNT* 3:496–87, esp. 476.

means subjecting God to πειρασμός. It certainly is this in the biblical Massah tradition, which, as I am arguing, is the background for much of the Disciple's Prayer. It is specifically what Paul envisages when he exhorts the Corinthians to avoid ἐπιθυμητὰς κακῶν (see 1 Cor. 10:9!). And in the light of Jesus' identification in Matt. 12:39 and Matt. 16:4, where Jesus identifies those among Israel who, having seen God's mighty works in Jesus, still seek proof that God is, as Jesus' claims, in their midst, as γενεὰ πονηρὰ καὶ μοιχαλὶς (see Matt. 12:45), thus recalling the "testing" themes in Exodus 17; Numbers 14; Psalms 78; 95, "evil" means "putting God to the test" according to Jesus as well. So, if τοῦ πονηροῦ here means "(doing) evil," then to be "delivered" ἀπὸ τοῦ πονηροῦ is also to be protected from putting God to the test.

If, then, the phrase ἀλλὰ ῥῦσαι ἡμᾶς ἀπὸ τοῦ πονηροῦ means, in fullest sense, "protect us from repeating the sin of Massah," "... from putting you [God] to the test," then we have yet another reason to think that the coordinate phrase καὶ μὴ εἰσενέγκῃς ἡμᾶς εἰς πειρασμόν originally meant, most fully, "prevent us, Father, from putting you to the test by doubting your ways and renouncing all that you have deemed fit for us to follow."

To sum up: In one section of his passionately rendered, and lamentably unfinished, *New Testament Theology* titled "What did Jesus expect?" Joachim Jeremias summed up all of his studies of the original meaning of the petition καὶ μὴ εἰσενέγκῃς ἡμᾶς εἰς πειρασμόν with the words: "The petition for protection from [entering into] πειρασμός is the desperate cry of faith on trial: preserve us from apostasy, keep us from going wrong."[62] The evidence I have examined in the preceding pages indicates that in this conclusion Jeremias is absolutely right. It *is* protection from "going wrong" that

---

62. *New Testament Theology*, 129.

is the intended object of the "temptation" request. But what we must also conclude, in the light of the evidence I have adduced above, that the nature of the "going wrong" envisaged in the petition is that of the particular sin Israel engaged in at Massah, the grumbling and the disobedience that was tantamount to "putting God to the test." Therefore, I submit that the original meaning of the "temptation" request is understood only when we see that καὶ μὴ εἰσενέγκῃς ἡμᾶς εἰς πειρασμόν was intended to be taken as a cry in which the community of believers asks to be protected by God not from experiencing πειρασμός, but from subjecting God to it.

If this conclusion is correct, it remains for me to say something regarding how, according to Jesus, being "led into testing," and consequently engaging in the activity of "proving God," would be fleshed out. What, in Jesus' eyes, might the community of believers whom he has called to be "sons of God" actually do that would be the functional equivalent of Israel's sin at Massah? The answer to this question seems clear enough given all that I have said about Jesus' understanding of what being faithful "sons" entails. The community would be rejecting the call from Jesus that it should regard as "of God," and therefore be bound by, the principle of nonretaliation and especially the constraint to love the enemy. For, as we have seen, a posture of nonretaliation and the willingness to love the enemy are together the epitome and the essence of the way that the community of Jesus' disciples has been charged to show itself faithful to the God it acknowledges as Father. This is what Jesus declares the disciples must commit themselves to if they are to be acknowledged by God as "sons." This is the way of God that "this generation," the antitype of the community Jesus tries to form, refuses to accept as the path God has ordained for those of Israel to follow. And, as I have shown elsewhere,[63] this is the path of obedience that is presumed and identified, in the story of Jesus' wilderness confrontation with the devil, as what a son must uphold as God's way in the world in order to avoid "putting God to the test."

---

63. Gibson, *Temptations of Jesus in Early Christianity*, 109–10.

Conclusion

So where are we? Have we been able to establish what Jesus meant his disciples to be praying for when they prayed the prayer he gave them? I believe we have, if somewhat indirectly. But first, before I lay out more directly what this is, let's summarize what we've discovered about the prayer itself.

- The Disciples' Prayer is indeed a prayer—a heartfelt attempt at communication with someone who is believed to support, maintain, and control the existence of the ones who engage in it; an act of communication is intended to have some effect on the one to whom it is addressed.
- It is a petitionary prayer.
- It is Jewish in character inasmuch as the one addressed in the prayer is the God of Israel and it reflects the beliefs of a people who knew that they were in a covenantal relationship with this God and therefore were expected to show themselves as faithful to what this God required of them.
- It is grounded in what the originator of the prayer, Jesus of Nazareth, had come to understand was the public expression of the particular path of faithfulness that God required of his people.

- It was not "eschatological" in orientation in the sense that its aim is not to pray down into the "now" things that properly belong to an anticipated "end time."

- Like all other prayers that Jesus urged his disciples to pray (and that he himself prayed), its aim from start to finish was to keep his band of disciples from straying from that path through their securing divine aid to help them remain faithful to God's ways as Jesus understood them.

Additionally, the data in the preceding chapter indicate that the traditional scholarly division of the prayer into a series of "you petitions" and "we petitions" is grounded in a misunderstanding of the aim of the prayer. Each of the constituent elements of the Disciples' Prayer after the invocation is a mixture of both "you" and "we" requests insofar as each of them asks God to do something for the disciples.

So what did Jesus intend his disciples to be asking for or saying when they recited the prayer he gave them? To answer this, I resort to paraphrase:

(Father)

We recognize that you alone are sovereign, and we pledge our loyalty to you even if this becomes costly for us.

(May your name be hallowed)

Protect us from dishonoring you through disobedience to your ways; enable us to remain true υἱοὶ θεοῦ even at the cost of our lives.

(May your kingdom come/May your Holy Spirit come upon us and cleanse us)

Shape us and maintain us as your people. Enable us to do your will.

(Do give/go on giving us our ἐπιούσιον bread)

Do not allow us to become like the wilderness generation, who grew dissatisfied with your ways and doubted your will to protect them and bring them to their destiny.

(Forgive us our sins [or debts] as we have forgiven those who have sinned against especially to out enemies.

We are intent to show the mercy you require υἱοὶ θεοῦ to show to those who have wronged us; and you may reject us if we do not.

(And do not lead us into πειρασμός)

And do not allow us to do what the wilderness generation did at Meribah and Massah and put you to the test, especially by denying that the way of the peacemaker, the εἰρηνηποιός, is truly your way of achieving your goals for the word.

People of faith pray to God for a variety of things: for relief from misery, for obtaining health and wealth, for a good grade or an easy test, for a sunny day, a victory, for rain, for the well-being of family, friends, and nation, and so on. In one way, there is nothing wrong with this, given their belief that God controls the world and that they and others are the object of God's love and concern. But if we take seriously the notion of the Disciples' Prayer as in any way a "model prayer"—that it not only shows what our petitionary prayers should be but also shapes our understanding of what being a υἱοὶ θεοῦ entails—then we must realize that most of the petitionary prayers orants of the prayer say, including their versions of the Disciples' Prayer, are not "true to form." More often than not, our petitionary prayers are aimed at changing God or getting God to modify or hurry up fulfilling what we presume to be his plans for the world (which, if we are honest with ourselves, are often closely identified with our own hopes for ourselves and those we identify with, especially in times of war and national crises). Or, to paraphrase Jesus' words in Gethsemane, we try to get God to do or to bring what we desire at any given time. But the Disciples' Prayer indicates that the aim of petitionary prayer should be to ask God to change us, not him, and to ensure that we are always conformed to, and satisfied with, his will, not our own.

Nor, it seems, judging by standard expositions of the Disciples' Prayer, is the "ordinary" sense of what people of faith are up to when they recite the Disciples' Prayer and address God as (our) Father consistent with Jesus' intentions. More often than not, those who pray the prayer seem to think that the purpose of praying it is to bring oneself within the presence of the infinite, the all-encompassing, and the omnipotent, and to engender within oneself what Schleiermacher claimed was at the core of being truly "religious," namely, a sense of awe and of absolute dependence on a higher power. But the Disciples' Prayer tells us otherwise. To profess God as Father entails taking a stance, not conjuring up emotion—and a particular stance at that, since to follow Jesus and say the Disciples' Prayer is to pledge oneself to demonstrating and proclaiming a certain way of "being" in the world, a way that mirrors and magnifies the very character of the God of Israel as Jesus has made him known. As Jesus declared according to Matthew's Gospel, "Not everyone who says to me, 'Lord, Lord,' shall enter the kingdom of heaven, but he who does the will of my Father who is in heaven." Consider how this is fleshed out in the story of judgment in Matthew 25.

> When the Son of man comes in his glory, and all the angels with him, then he will sit on his glorious throne. Before him will be gathered all the nations, and he will separate them one from another as a shepherd separates the sheep from the goats, and he will place the sheep at his right hand, but the goats at the left. Then the King will say to those at his right hand, "Come, O blessed of my Father, inherit the kingdom prepared for you from the foundation of the world; for I was hungry and you gave me food, I was thirsty and you gave me drink, I was a stranger

and you welcomed me, I was naked and you clothed me, I was sick and you visited me, I was in prison and you came to me." Then the righteous will answer him, "Lord, when did we see thee hungry and feed thee, or thirsty and give thee drink? And when did we see thee a stranger and welcome thee, or naked and clothe thee? And when did we see thee sick or in prison and visit thee?" And the King will answer them, "Truly, I say to you, as you did it to one of the least of these my brethren, you did it to me." Then he will say to those at his left hand, "Depart from me, you cursed, into the eternal fire prepared for the devil and his angels; for I was hungry and you gave me no food, I was thirsty and you gave me no drink, I was a stranger and you did not welcome me, naked and you did not clothe me, sick and in prison and you did not visit me." Then they also will answer, "Lord, when did we see thee hungry or thirsty or a stranger or naked or sick or in prison, and did not minister to thee?" Then he will answer them, "Truly, I say to you, as you did it not to one of the least of these, you did it not to me." And they will go away into eternal punishment, but the righteous into eternal life (Matt. 25:31-46 RSV).

Appendix: Was John the Baptist the Author of the Disciples' Prayer?

As we have seen above, the majority of scholars who have dealt with the question of whether the Disciples' Prayer originates with Jesus have followed ancient tradition and answered in the affirmative, even if they think that what is presented in Matthew and Luke and the Didache is, in form and wording, an expansion, recasting, or compilation of words that Jesus spoke to his disciples.[1] But a small number of exegetes claim that the actual author of the prayer was not Jesus. Rather, it was the prophetic figure with whom Jesus initially associated himself before embarking on his own ministry, John the Baptizer. Exemplary here is Joan Taylor who offers two main arguments.

The first is that it is quite clear from Lk. 11:2 that Jesus' disciples actually wanted him to do things as John did in relation to *his* disciples. One of them is recorded as saying, "Master, teach us to pray as John taught his disciples" (Luke 11:1), and Jesus then responds by teaching them "the Lord's Prayer." Now, since the offering of prayers

---

1. See Hans Dieter Betz, *The Sermon on the Mount: A Commentary on the Sermon on the Mount, Including the Sermon on the Plain (Matthew 5:3—7:27 and Luke 6:20-49)*, ed. Adela Yarbro Collins (Minneapolis: Fortress Press, 1995), 372 n332.

THE DISCIPLES' PRAYER

is considered characteristic of John's disciples in Luke 5:33, and since as the *LSJ*[2] and such New Testament texts as Matt. 21:6[3] and Matt. 26:24[4] show, καθώς can mean "just as" or "exactly as."

Thus, while the common interpretation of Lk. 11:1 is that Jesus was asked to teach his disciples a short prayer in the same general sort of way that John taught his disciples a (different) short prayer. "Equally, however, it could be that the disciples wanted exactly the same prayer as that taught by John to his disciples. Therefore, we may consider this prayer one that just might have been taught by John."[5]

Second, a prayer such as we find at Lk. 11:2-4—with its focus on an imminent coming of God's kingdom and his rule on earth, when the righteous will live and the unrighteous perish, and its emphases on the forgiveness of sins (which ensured purity of heart) and a repentant spirit—fits well with the eschatalogical message of John and places it in the same theological tradition from which John arose and in which he steeped himself.[6]

But is she correct? Few (including myself) have thought so. For there are several problems with her arguments. First, while καθώς *can* mean "exactly as" (see Luke 24:25), the adverb was also used to indicate an analogy or a general comparison, not an exact correspondence between one thing and another.[7] So we would need

---

2. *LSJ*, 857.
3. "The disciples went and did exactly as (καθώς) Jesus had told them."
4. "But the son of humankind/the man goes exactly as (καθώς) it has been written of him."
5. Joan Taylor, *The Immerser: John the Baptist in Jewish Tradition* (Grand Rapids: Eerdmans, 1996), 151–52.
6. Taylor, *The Immerser*, 153.
7. I find it curious that to support her linguistic claim, Taylor not only appeals to the standard Lexicon for Classical Greek, the *LSJ* (Henry George Liddell, Robert Scott, Henry Stuart Jones, and Roderick McKenzie, *A Greek-English Lexicon*, 9th ed., with revised supplement [Oxford: Clarendon, 1996], 857), rather than to the standard one for New Testament Greek (Frederick W. Danker, Walter Bauer, William F. Arndt, and F. Wilbur Gingrich, eds., *Greek English Lexicon of the Greek New Testament and Other Early Christian Literature*, 3rd ed. [Chicago: University of Chicago Press, 2000) and to texts in Matthew that, according to her, use καθώς with the sense of "exactly as" (though the translators of the EV, the RSV, and the NIV do not see the adverb as bearing this sense there, rendering it instead with "as" [EV, RSV] or "just as" [NIV] in

APPENDIX

more evidence than Taylor (and others[8]) offer to accept that it does actually mean "just as"/"exactly as" here.

Second, her claim that it is equally likely that what Jesus was asked to do was to teach his disciples the same prayer John taught to his disciples as it is that Jesus was asked to teach his disciples a short prayer that was different from John's is really nothing more than an assertion, even should we grant that καθώς in Luke 11:1 means "exactly as." Why should we believe, as it seems we must if we are to see Taylor's claim as valid, that the referent of καθώς is John's prayer rather than his act of giving his disciples something that helped not only to characterize them as his but also to set them apart from other groups within Judaism.[9]

The third has to do with Taylor's claim about how well the concerns of the prayer fit with the message of John as she reconstructs it. As we will see below, there is good reason to call into question, if not reject, the notion that the Disciples' Prayer is eschatological in nature. And if it is not, then the claimed fit between what the prayer is concerned with and "the theological tradition" in which John took part may be more apparent than real.

Fourth, the greatest problem with this view arises from a fact that Taylor herself acknowledges as true, namely, that a number of Jesus' disciples had been disciples of John.[10] Why would any disciple, let alone one who presumably had not been one of John's followers, ask

---

both instances) rather than to Lukan usage of the adverb, but, more importantly, misrepresents what is found in the LSJ under its entry on καθώς—to wit:

καθώς Adv. = καθά, Hdt. 9.82 codd., Arist. *Pr.* 891b34, *IG* 5(2).344.20 (*Arc.*, iii b.c.), Wilcken *Chr.* 11 A 53 (ii b.c.), IG 22.1030.22 (i b.c.), al.; *even as*, *Ev.Jo.* 15.12.

2. how, ὑπομιμνῄσκειν κ. Aristeas 263, cf. Act.Ap. 15.12. II. of Time, as, when, ib.7.17, LXX 2 Ma. 1.31, Aristeas 310. (Condemned by Phryn. 397, Moer. 212.).

8. See Clare K. Rothschild, *Baptist Traditions and Q: The Dawn from on High* (Tübingen: Mohr Siebeck, 2005), 86–87.
9. As John Nolland notes, here "the disciples seek a prayer that will express the distinctive piety that Jesus' own life has expressed and into which he has drawn the disciple band" (*Luke 9:21–18:34*, Word Biblical Commentary [Dallas: Word, 1993], 611).
10. Taylor, *Immerser*, 152.

THE DISCIPLES' PRAYER

Jesus to teach the company of his disciples (see Luke 11:1, "teach us") a prayer that was already known among them?[11]

Given these observations, it seems clear that the case for John the Baptizer as the author of the Lord's Prayer has little to recommend it.

---

11. A question Taylor herself raises when she observes, "If others from his own close circle disciples, such as Peter and Andrew, were also once disciples of John [so John 1:35-42; cf. Acts 1:22], they also would have known the short prayer John taught and would undoubtedly have used it" (ibid., 153), but, notably, she doesn't answer!

Index

Allen, W. C., 26
Allison, D. C., 26, 103, 111, 116, 123–24, 126, 136, 155
Ambrozic, A., 77
Amidah, 50, 52, 54–57, 105–9
Anselm, 85
Apocalypse of Baruch, 121–22
apocalyptic expectation, 140
apostasy, 88–90, 94–97, 100, 103, 108, 113, 119, 133, 136, 141, 151, 158
Augustine, 9, 84
Aune, D., 122

Baba Batra, 112
Baptizer, 24–25, 63, 85, 88, 167, 170
Barclay, W., 38
Barnes, Albert, 36
Barr, J., 132
Barrett, C. K., 76
Bauer, W., 149, 156

Beale, G. K, 122
Beasley-Murray, G. R., 103
Beatitudes, 80, 116
Betz, H. D., 37, 63, 88, 111, 124, 136, 145–46, 167
Beyer, H. W., 76
Billerbeck, P., 56, 115
Black, C. C., 77
Black, M., 56
Blakely, J. T., 101
Blass, F., 117
Blenkinsopp, J., 156
Bock, D., 56, 97
Borg, M., 83
Bradshaw, P. F., 54–55
Brocke, M., 44, 49, 51, 61
Bromiley, G., 67, 123, 152
Brown, C., 45–46
Brown, R. E., 102–3, 106, 109, 114, 126, 135, 144, 150, 153
Brown, S., 140–41

Bultmann, Rudolf, 26, 102
Burney, C. F., 18–19, 26
Burridge, Richard, 64
Bussche, H., 37
Byargeon, R., 124

Caecilius, 2
Caird, G. B., vii, 65–66, 84, 86, 110, 112, 127, 136, 138
Calvin, 136
Carlson, Stephen, viii
Carmignac. J., 123, 135, 146, 153, 155
Carruth, S., 19
Chancey, M. A., 59
Charlesworth, J. H., 53, 59, 122
Chase, F. W., 155
Chilton, B., 111, 129
Chouinard, L., 36
Chrysostom, 13
Clarke, A., 35
Clement, 139
Conrad, Carl, viii
Conzelmann, H., 141
Crehan, J. H., 139
crisis, 24, 88, 117, 140–41, 151–52
cross, 64, 69–72, 75, 78, 89, 120, 154
Crossan, J. D., 22–24, 123
Crump, D., 28, 49, 55, 110, 120, 132–33

Cullmann, O., 89, 135, 145
Cyprian, 2, 14, 38, 136, 146
Cyster, R. F., 148

Dalman, G., 120
Danker, F. W., 11, 149, 168
Davies, W. D., 26, 103, 111, 116, 123–24, 126, 136, 155
Dawson, G., viii
death, 72, 84–85, 100–101, 112, 120
Debrunner, A., 117
debtor, 129
Derrett, J. D. M., 131
devil, 39, 143, 146, 156, 160
Didache, 2, 12–13, 19, 27, 63, 139, 167
discipleship, 43, 68, 97, 132
Doble, P., 8
Dunn, J. D. G., viii, 59
Dupont, J., 81

Eighteen Benedictions, 7, 50
Eisler, R., 102
Elliott, N., viii
Ellis, E., 103, 123
emperor, 20, 77, 133
enemy, love of, 81, 83–84, 130
enter, entering ("temptation"), 69, 153, 155, 158
enticement, 39, 143

eschatalogical, 37, 54, 90, 103–6, 108–11, 113–114, 116–17, 119–20, 126, 128–29, 132, 135, 137–38, 140–41, 145, 150, 162, 169
eschatologists, 109, 114, 116, 121–22, 124–27, 132, 138
eschatology, apocalyptic, 138
evil, 18, 24, 103, 157–58
evil (one), 10, 155, 157
exile, 118–19

faithfulness, 34, 39, 43–44, 66–67, 72, 86, 89, 95, 100, 108, 115, 138, 141–46, 151, 154–56, 161
Fanning, B., 109
Finkelstein, L., 107
Fitzmyer, J. A., 22, 56, 133
Fleischer, E., 54
Flesher, P. V. M., 59
Foerster, W., 79, 83, 123–24, 152
forgiveness, 10–12, 21, 23, 27, 37–38, 46, 52, 55, 60, 64, 69, 79–80, 84, 90, 123, 126–32, 168
Funk, R., 22, 117

Galilee, 59, 97
Gardner, R. B., 37, 39
Garsky, A., 19
Gebraud, B., 51

Geddert, T. J., 154
generation: this (wicked/adulterous), 25, 68–69, 87, 96–102, 104; wilderness, 98, 104, 121, 148, 152, 163
Gerhardsson, B., 34, 142–43, 147, 151–52
Gethsemane, 87, 89, 91, 100, 113, 164
Gibson, J. B., 160
Gill, J., 36
Gingrich, 11, 149, 168
Goodacre, M., viii
Goulder, M., 20–24, 26, 45–46, 63
Graubard, B., 44
Grayston, K., 153
greatness, 69, 72–73, 76–78
Greeven, H., 102
Gregory of Nyssa, 114
Griffiths, P. J., viii
Grundmann, W., 77, 157
Guelich, R., 81, 83
Gundry, R., 94, 140

Haenchen, E., 58
Hagner, D. A., 103
hallowing, 9, 36, 115, 119–20, 132
Hammer, R., 115
Harder, G., 156–57
Harding, M., 53
Harnack, A. von, 9, 123, 136

Harrington, D. J., 49
Heller, J., 135
Hengel, M., 115
Herzog, W., 131–32
Hicks, J. M., 42
Higgins, A. J. B., 146
Hill, D. A., 78, 156
Hooker, M. D., 76
Horsley, R. A., 56–57, 66, 137
Houk, H., 148, 153
hypocrites, 68, 88, 96

Iverson, K., 101

Jeremias, J., 15–16, 18–20, 26, 49, 54, 56, 102–3, 106, 114, 116, 126, 135–36, 143, 146, 150, 155, 158
Jerome, 136, 146
Jewett, R., vii
Jones, H. S., 168
Josephus, 49, 57, 59, 77
justice, 65, 78, 84, 103, 111

Kaddish, 51, 54–57, 59–62, 105–9, 117
Kaylor, R. D., 66
Kelber, W., 78
Keller, W. P., 35–37, 42
Kingdom of God, 24, 37, 110, 150
Kingsbury, J. D., 67

Kloppenborg, J., 23, 67
Knox, R., 110
Korn, J. H., 33, 147–55
Kuhn, K. G., 154

Lane, W. L., 78, 154
Leaney, R., 9
Leroe, B., 36
Levine, L., 54, 56–57
Liddell, H. G., 168
Lierman, J., 7
Lightfoot, R. H., 59, 156–57
Lohmeyer, E., 19, 102, 136, 144, 150, 155
Lövestam, E., 97
Lührmann, D., 81
Luz, U., 26, 115, 117, 136, 138, 140

Malina, B., 46, 130
Manson, T. W., 155
Marcion, 114, 123, 136, 146
Marshall, I. H., 55–56, 136–37, 141
Martin, T., viii
martyrdom, 72, 120
Massah, 68, 148–59
McGrath, J., viii
McKenzie, R., 168
McKnight, S., 66, 132–33
McNeil, A. H., 27

Meadors, E. P., 66
Meecham, G., 153
Meier, J. P., 102, 106, 111, 116, 120
Meribah, 68, 163
Metzger, B. M., 14
Milavec, A., 27
Millar, F., 56
Mishnah, 8, 51
Moore, G. F., 112
Morgan, R., viii
Moule, C. F. D., 136, 140, 143–46
Muddiman, J., viii

Nickelsburg, G. W. E, 122
Niederwimmer, K., 2, 19, 27
Nolland, J., 56, 58, 95, 108, 169
nonretaliation, 83, 159

Oakman, D., 123
obedience, path of, 44, 159
offense, 90, 129–30
Origen, 14, 37–38, 136

peacemaker, 69, 80–83, 163
peasant, 23
Pendry, P., viii
Perrin, N., 103
persecution, 39, 72, 84, 96, 115, 134, 136–37, 141
Pervo, R., viii

petitionary prayer, 47–48, 88–89, 163
Pink, A., 36, 38
Piper, J., 83
Pitre, B., 18, 25, 112–13, 136
Plummer, A., 88
Porter, S., 14, 109, 135
prayer: eschatological, 53, 105, 109; Jewish, 46–52
preservation, 38–39, 103, 108
profane/profanation, 36, 49, 98, 115, 117–19

Raynal, G., viii
Reike, B., 97
Reimer, J., viii
remnant, 25, 67, 113
retaliate/retaliation, 66, 80, 83–84, 130
righteous/righteousness, 111–12
Robbins, V. K., 18
Robinson, J. T., 7
Rothschild, C., 169

sabbath, 45, 50, 94
sanctify/sanctifying, 98, 115–17, 119–20
Sanders, E. P., 57–58
Satan/satanic, 89, 100, 102, 136, 144, 157
Schedler, N., viii

Schleiermacher, F., 164
Schlier, H., 72
Schmidt, K. L., 86
Schniewind, J., 144, 156
Schulz, S., 103
Schürer, E., 56
Schürmann, H., 56, 102, 156
Schwarz, G., 19
Schweitzer, Albert, 102
Schweizer, Eduard, 67, 116–17, 145, 156
Scott, E. F., 9, 18, 27–28
Seesemann, H., 141, 147, 151, 153, 155
servant, 76, 112, 120, 130–32, 153
Shemoneh Esreh, 7, 50, 54, 56
sin(s), 11, 15, 28, 38, 40, 84, 103, 123, 126
sinner, 36, 76, 90, 126, 128–29
Smith, C. F. W., 144–45
son(s) of God, 44, 67, 69, 71, 80, 83–84, 86, 94, 96, 148, 159
Spence-Jones, H. D. M., 38
Spicq, C. S., 143
Stein, D. E., 115
Stein, R. H., 15
Steinhaeuser, A. T. W., 38
Stendahl, K., 154
Stevenson, K., 42
Strack, H. L., 115
Streeter, B. H., 9

Sykes, M. H., 145, 155
synagogue, 51, 54–59, 62, 64, 91, 95

Talmud, 50–51, 54, 127
Targum, 129–30
Taussig, H., 23
Taylor, J., 167–70
temptation, 31–34, 38–39, 46, 52, 55, 68, 89, 100, 132, 135–36, 140–41, 143, 145–47, 149–50, 152–53, 155–56, 159
test/testing, 10–11, 20, 24, 28, 33, 39, 46, 52, 68, 94, 98, 103, 108, 122, 136, 138–51, 154–56, 158–60, 163
Thurston, H., 2
torah reading, 50, 57
Trench, R. C., 149
trial(s), 30, 39–40, 94, 100, 102, 115, 123, 136–37, 139, 141, 144–45, 151, 158
tribulation, great/time of, 103, 135–37, 141, 143

Urman, D., 59

vengeance, 58, 76
Vermes, G., 56
Vögtle, A., 103, 123

Waetjen, H. C., 39–40
Weiss, J., 102, 138
wicked/wickedness, 10, 68, 83, 127, 130, 132, 134, 151, 157
wilderness, 11, 45–46, 68, 97–98, 123, 148, 150, 156, 159
wilderness generation, 98, 104, 121, 148, 152, 163
Williams, T., viii

Willis, G. G., 137, 146
Windisch, H., 67, 82–83
Wright, N. T., 65–66, 86, 122, 127

Yoder, J. H., 71

Zahn, T. H., 102
Zeitlin, S., 54

www.ingramcontent.com/pod-product-compliance
Lightning Source LLC
Chambersburg PA
CBHW071202070526
44584CB00019B/2890